GHOST STORIES
of OREGON

D0188658

Susan Smitten

GHOST HOUSE

Ghost House Books

© 2001 by Ghost House Books
First printed in 2001 10 9 8 7 6 5 4 3 2 1
Printed in Canada

The Publisher: Ghost House Books
Distributed by Lone Pine Publishing
10145 – 81 Avenue
Edmonton, AB T6E 1W9
Canada
Website: http://www.ghostbooks.net

National Library of Canada Cataloguing in Publication Data
Smitten, Susan, 1961–
  Ghost Stories of Oregon
ISBN 1–894877–13–6

  1. Ghosts—Oregon. 2. Legends—Oregon. I. Title.
GR580.S68 2002   398.2'0979505   C2002–910539–0

Editorial Director: Nancy Foulds
Editorial: Shelagh Kubish, Chris Wrangler, Volker Bodegom
Illustrations Coordinator: Carol Woo
Production Coordinator: Jennifer Fafard
Cover Design: Gerry Dotto
Layout and Production: Jeff Fedorkiw
Photo Credits: Every effort has been made to accurately credit photographers. Any errors or omissions should be directed to the publisher for changes in future editions. The photographs in this book are reproduced with the kind permission of the following sources: McMenamins Pubs and Breweries (p. 9, 130, 133, 136, 140, 143, 147, 149, 153, 157, 163, 171, 187); National Archives, Pacific–Alaska Region (p. 15, NRIS–26–AIDSTONAVPHO–TILLROCK1); Michael P. Jones (p. 26); National Archives, Still Pictures Branch (p. 32, NWDNS–79–OC–20); Geiser Grand Hotel (p. 37, 39, 44); Oregon Historical Society (p. 55, OrHi–39576); Sunriver Resort (p. 65); Southern Oregon Historical Society (p. 71, #6991; p. 99, #1236); Clatsop County Historical Society (p. 77, #2337); Oregon Vortex (p. 81); Yaquina Bay Lighthouse (p. 88); Library of Congress (p. 96, HABS, ORE, 15–JACVI, 21–1); Ingrid Painter (p. 109); Pittock Mansion (p. 94, 116); Fort Dalles Museum (p. 121); Richard Davis (p. 176); Glenbow Archives (p. 200, NA–1194–14); Oregon State Historic Preservation Office (p. 210, Jeff Lohr).

The stories, folklore and legends in this book are based on the author's collection of sources including individuals whose experiences have led them to believe they have encountered phenomena of some kind or another. They are meant to entertain, and neither the publisher nor the author claims these stories represent fact.

We acknowledge the financial support of the Government of Canada through the Book Publishing Industry Development Program (BPIDP) for our publishing activities.

PC: P5

Dedication

For my wonderful parents, Iris and Allan, whose love and support made this book possible.

Contents

Chapter Four: Haunted Houses

Chapter Five: Spectral Snippets

Chapter Six: The McMenamins' Paranormal Empire

Chapter Seven: Spirits of Schools and Stages

Chapter Eight: Oregon City's Haunted History

Acknowledgments

A surprising number of people contributed to the content of this book. My thanks from start to finish extend to: Shane Kennedy, for his belief that underneath my television-producer exterior beat the heart of a writer; the rest of the Ghost House team for guiding me along a well-worn path and helping me to avoid the obvious pitfalls; Oregon's paranormal societies and researchers, who have made my job so much easier by digging up the incredible stories and histories that make up the bulk of the state's haunted memoirs; the librarians and library research assistants—bless every one of them—who not only keep "ghost files" but will dig them out of dusty vaults; the members of the Oregon Historical Society and Southern Oregon Historical Society; and pretty much every manager at McMenamins' haunted establishments, with special mention to Tim Hills, the staff historian whose detailed work chronicles much of Oregon's rich, working-class history. My heartfelt thanks also go to editors Shelagh, Chris and Volker for sculpting these stories. Finally, I would like to offer special thanks to all those who took the time to share their experiences.

Introduction

I was excited by the prospect of gathering ghost stories from such a beautiful and distinct state. But I must confess that I didn't know what to expect at first. Would people have stories to tell? Could I expect them to listen when I mentioned the word "ghost?" Or would they just laugh out loud? The answers are yes, no and—once again—yes.

Oregon's ghost stories, which go back hundreds of years, are not limited to creepy old houses. Native Americans used them to instruct rather than to frighten. Ghost stories were legends with a moral, not the bump-in-the-night tales that prevail today. When the pioneers arrived, many met ghosts. Some heard ghostly canoes when the fog settled over the Willamette River or saw Native American spirits in creek bottoms. As the frontier changed, some towns became ghost towns, abandoned by everyone except spirits of dead settlers and prospectors.

Today, ghost stories are as plentiful as ever. In northwestern Oregon, where a craggy and forbidding coastline juts into the Pacific Ocean, almost every lighthouse is haunted by ghosts or ghastly goings-on. In some cases, the line between fact and fiction has become blurred, as in Lischen M. Miller's short story of Muriel Trevenard, who many believe haunts Newport's Yaquina Bay Lighthouse. One man, who laughed at me when I asked about a ghost in his family history, told me that his father once went into the local lighthouse and made noises to scare passersby. This is one case in which the power of suggestion may supersede the powers of observation.

But many of the stories I collected were corroborated by people with firsthand experiences. Oregon's universities, for example, have their own share of ghosts, including Vera,

Pacific University's most longstanding undergraduate, said to stalk Knight Hall. After a frightening Ouija board session in the hall, one group of people became convinced that Vera was a bona fide presence. Public schools and theaters also have a surprising number of visitors who don't require a hall pass or ticket. Just ask the faculty or students at Western Oregon University about the ghost of George Harding. And was that Charles Laughton's apparition lurking backstage at the Ashland Shakespeare Festival?

Some of the state's founding fathers have a hard time leaving the running of things to the earthbound. Dr. John McLoughlin, the reputed "Father of Oregon," died in 1857, but his presence is still felt by those who work in his historic home in Oregon City. Henry Pittock, no less, regularly sends messages from beyond the grave to the people working in the public museum that once was his home.

Oregon also has a mystery spot where gravity itself seems to be warped. Perceptions of up, down, straight and crooked are confused by what some people say are powerful gravitational anomalies and dizzying magnetic vortexes. Is that really the case, or are our senses being fooled by artificial and natural optical illusions? You'll have to visit Gold Hill to find out.

And then there are the haunted McMenamin properties. It's astounding that two beer-brewing brothers, Mike and Brian, can be so consistent at divining phantoms. Ghosts are said to become more active during restoration projects, so that may explain why nearly a dozen of the brothers' properties feature a spirit or two. The same goes for Oregon's many haunted hotels, houses and public spaces, where a combination of history, tragedy and renovation make for an occasionally terrifying encounter with an otherworldly presence.

The Thompson Brewery and Public House, one of the many haunted buildings in the McMenamin brothers' hospitality empire

• • •

What is a ghost? One dictionary defines it as "the spirit of a dead person, especially one believed to appear in bodily likeness to living persons or to haunt former habitats." It goes on to say a ghost is a demon or spirit. But the truth is, no one really knows exactly what a ghost is.

Hauntings are similar. Thousands of reports from all over the world leave little doubt that haunting experiences are real, but who can say for certain whether a haunting has or has not occurred? One definition says it is the repeated manifestation of strange and inexplicable sensory phenomena—smells, sounds, tactile sensations and hallucinations—said to be caused by ghosts or spirits attached to a certain locale. But what causes a haunting is unknown.

Traditional theories about ghosts suggest they are spirits of dead people that for some reason are trapped in this plane of existence. The view is that some tragedy or trauma keeps them stuck here. Or there may be unfinished business that prevents movement to the next dimension. Many paranormal experts and ghost hunters believe ghosts aren't even aware that they are dead.

Existing in limbo, ghosts haunt the scenes of their deaths or return to locations that were pleasant to them when alive. Some ghosts are able to interact with the living and are aware of their surroundings; they can respond to those who see them when they materialize. Other ghosts seem to be mere recordings, like well-worn grooves in time, that return to play out a scene over and over in the environment where they once existed. These ghosts do not interact with anyone and may be unaware of the living. Their appearance never varies and their actions are always the same. They are like residual energy—traces of someone or something that once was but is long gone. Why such ghostly recordings are made, or why a spirit plays out a scene repetitiously, is unclear.

The most common kind of ghost is a messenger that arrives soon after a death either to comfort loved ones or to deliver a final message. These ghosts usually appear only once and vanish. Once the spirit has communicated with the chosen person—usually to let him or her know that there is no reason to grieve—it moves on.

Poltergeists are the most feared phantoms of the spirit world. They can actually affect the physical environment, causing unexplained banging, thumping, screeching, creaking, slamming and wailing. Poltergeists hide things, turn lights on and off, lock doors and toss things around. The word "poltergeist" comes from the German *poltern*, "to knock," and *geist*, "spirit." Generally, this type of spirit is connected to a child, although some poltergeists exist without a child around. Some paranormal experts believe a poltergeist is the spirit of a child or an insane adult. And though some poltergeists are harmless, others are decidedly mean-spirited manifestations that pull hair, slap faces and take pleasure in tormenting the living.

Ghosts don't always show themselves in the form of a dead person, animal or inanimate object. As the activity near the village of Rhododendron makes clear, ghostly phenomena can take the form of a mist or light. The gray mist or vapor that floats above the ground is also referred to as ecto-plasm. It is usually seen outdoors, especially around cemeteries and historical sites.

Bright spots of yellow or white light called "orbs" are another common sighting. The orbs are considered a convenient way for spirits to travel. Often, ghost hunters capture the hovering balls of energy on film or video, though many purported orb photos have been the result of a camera malfunction or some environmental circumstance. Orbs generally appear at night, and for that reason they show up well in photographs. It is possible that the orbs may not be associated with humans at all, but rather with living plant energy—from trees, for example—that accumulates and shows up as light.

The skeptic's view, of course, is that ghosts are pure invention. Many people who shared their experiences with me admitted that they might have fallen victim to the power of suggestion. The human mind is powerful, so it is possible that people see what they need to see, even if they have to unconsciously create it themselves. Given how little we know of the mind's true capabilities, it is possible that someone with a firm enough belief in ghosts or a spirit world could actually create a physical projection.

So are there such things as ghosts? I have only ever been on the receiving end of ghost stories. But because I have heard so many compelling and inexplicable tales from reasonable people, I have to say I just don't know—but I do accept that there's more to life that what can be seen, smelled, felt or heard.

I hope this collection is entertaining, amusing and sometimes chilling. I have presented people's stories as they recounted them, letting the events speak for themselves. I have also tried to provide historical context where it seemed necessary, appropriate or just plain interesting.

One final thought—if these stories motivate you to visit some of the places mentioned, be aware that many of them are either private property or historical sites. In each case, and particularly with cemeteries, please be respectful.

1

Coast and Wilderness Ghosts

The Phantom Ship

With a coast as rugged and ominous as the Pacific Northwest's, it's surprising that there aren't more accounts of ghost ships seeking safe harbor near Tillamook Rock. Many a vessel met its end during the awesome storms that lashed Oregon's coast.

One of Tillamook Rock's lighthouse keepers kept track of his experiences during his year of service. James Gibbs wrote of one night in particular when he and his three mates watched a decrepit ship drift dangerously close to rocks that would instantly dash it to pieces. Gibbs was awakened by his fellow lighthouse keepers' shouts and he leapt out of bed and got dressed. He writes:

I was outside in a flash and Swede was waiting for me, all wrought up as if his blood was boiling in his veins. He pointed to the dim outline of a vessel parting the strands of mist less than a quarter of a mile away, its dull gray silhouette blending with the sky and sea and hinting of mystery.

Through the glass one could tell that she was an old steamer that boasted a chronicle of long and hectic years—her seams had opened and the oakum had baked out through a series of summers. Badly hogged, her decks had grown sodden from rain and sea water, and the rigging hung limp from her fore and main mast like a broken spider web against the dismal sky. The dingy paint was peeling from her sides, and streaks of rust from iron fittings had left tell tale marks. The davits swung empty, the pilot house was partly stove in and the cabin portholes creaked open and shut with the pulse of the ocean.

From high atop Tillamook Rock, James Gibbs and his mates once saw a doomed ship vanish inexplicably.

Gibbs and his crewmates radioed the closest Coast Guard cutter, but there was no way to reach the drifting ship before it smashed into the rocks. The men peered closely but could see no sign of life on board, no one to steer the ship safely past Tillamook Rock. They steeled themselves for the inevitable, but Gibbs' account continues with a shocking outcome.

In the clutches of destruction, a stone's throw away, she became almost motionless in a vicious tide rip that knifed about her hull. She then spun about as though some skillful navigator had taken the helm, but her stern stuck momentarily, dislodging a bulky wooden rudder, which drifted free as she squeezed by the perilous southwest corner by a gnat's eyebrow. We could have spit on her decks as she passed below us in her death agonies. It was almost supernatural. Spared from disaster, that sinister derelict pursued her ghostly course until she had vanished in the northwesterly mists on her capricious voyage to nowhere.

No ship or wreckage was ever found. The Coast Guard scoured the area and found nothing.

But on one stormy night, not long after the sighting, the lighthouse crew noticed a piece of wood lodged in the rocks on the lower platform. They shone a light on it, and realized it was an ancient rudder, like the wooden one that had come off the derelict vessel. Although it was dangerous to retrieve it in such bad weather, the men felt compelled to try. James Gibbs was lowered by a rope and came within a few feet of the rudder but at that moment a massive wave shook the coast, nearly killing Gibbs and taking the rudder back out to sea.

The rudder disappeared into the swirling foam. Gibbs and his fellow keepers were left to wonder if they had shared a late-night hallucination or if they had actually seen a phantom ship.

John Day Crossing

Just east of Wasco in Grant County, where the Oregon Trail once crossed the John Day River, the greed of the gold rush got to one couple who ran a ferry and hotel. According to some, the wife's avarice keeps her coming back to the banks of the river in search of a treasure that could be miles downstream by now.

Mary and Daniel Leonard made a living running a ferry service to take people across the river in the days before bridges. They provided accommodations for newly wealthy prospectors in their hotel. Gold was discovered in Canyon Creek in 1862, and during the following gold rush, over $26 million in gold was mined in the John Day–Canyon City area. The rocks and earth of Eastern Oregon and Montana yielded $140 million in the boom years between 1861 and 1867. Farmers stampeded to the mines in search of the precious metal, while prospectors pored over every river, lake, mountain and plain hoping to stake a claim. Compared to the primitive lives of the early pioneers, gold seekers struck it rich in record numbers. They euphorically flaunted their newfound wealth by drinking and eating well, staying at hotels, and gambling in high-stakes poker games.

During that time, rumor has it that the Leonards murdered several of their patrons for their gold and money. They disposed of the bodies and buried the loot near the river. Several years passed, and the couple's happy union dissolved into acrimony. During one confrontation, Mary apparently killed her husband. She was never convicted of the crime. But freedom came with a price. Mary could never find the treasure and eventually left the area. A ghost wearing a long dress was seen some years later floating through the rooms of the stage station. The station was torn down in the mid-1950s, but locals say the ghost of Mary Leonard often returns to the bank of the John Day River to search for her buried booty.

The Creepy Catacombs of West Linn

It's not surprising that the oldest operating sawmill in the Pacific Northwest has a ghost or two. Hidden underneath the West Linn Paper Mill is a large cavelike room known to locals as "the catacombs." The muddy floors are constantly damp from the water that seeps down the walls from the Willamette River. And although the cellar is empty, there are some who say mill workers from long ago continue to show up for work.

The town's founder, Robert Moore, settled the area in the early 1840s after buying 1,000 acres of land from the Wallamut Indians. Despite the rugged topography, he built his cabin on a slope overlooking the Willamette Falls, across the river from Oregon City. Moore set about developing a town that he called Robin's Nest. Within six years he had four flour and lumber mills, and he ran a ferry across to Oregon City. In 1845, Moore renamed Robin's Nest to Linn City in honor of his friend, Senator Lewis Linn of Missouri.

Continually expanding his empire, Robert Moore built another flour mill on Moore Island in the 1850s. Not long after Moore's death in 1857, a devastating fire destroyed the mill. Local businessmen rebuilt it only to see their work, along with most of Linn City, washed away in the terrible flood of 1860. The town, renamed West Linn, was rebuilt again. On Moore Island, the catacombs were carved out of the rock to serve as a basement for the next flour mill.

After the flour mill closed, the underground area served as a convenient storage area for logs when the Willamette Pulp and Paper Company opened the first paper mill on the location in 1888. Throughout the early decades of operation, conditions on the job were dangerous. Accidents were common and pay was low. Many an employee lost an arm in the mill. Workers put in grueling eleven-hour shifts, seven days a week.

Time and technology advanced. The mill went through several owners and in 1997 it became part of the West Linn Paper Company, a subsidiary of Vancouver-based Belgravia Investments Limited. In the early 1990s, the mill converted from acid to alkaline papermaking, which meant better quality paper and big operational changes. The basement area went through several changes, shifting from storage to processing. Grinder rooms were set up with giant machines to grind logs into wood pulp. More advancements in pulp processing resulted in shutting the basement area down. The grinder rooms are now empty. Except, that is, for the ghosts who may not realize their services are no longer needed.

Phil Peterson used to run the janitorial business that contracted with the West Linn Paper Company. His connection to the mill goes back to the late 1940s when his grandmother worked there. During his time at the mill, Peterson experienced the odd cold chill up his spine when he would check out the catacombs, particularly in the abandoned restroom.

His most peculiar encounter, however, was in one of the old grinder rooms. In an interview with *Oregonian* reporter Dennis McCarthy, Peterson claims he heard strange voices and sounds coming from Grinder Room Two. Accompanied by a security guard, he once went into the room and heard male voices saying, "What time is it? Let's go home." Both Peterson and the security guard glanced at the clock on the wall, which read exactly five o'clock—quitting time. Only thing was, the clock was unplugged. The two looked at each other and bolted.

When asked about the ghost stories, the company's director of human resources was caught a little off guard. After more than 17 years working at West Linn, Ian Dunlap says his only knowledge of any ghosts was from the local newspaper story. There haven't been any ghost sightings or any other accounts of hearing voices or strange noises. When I spoke to Ian, he said the underground area has been shut down since 1990, so no one goes down there much any more. Could it be that some mill workers from long ago got stuck in a psychic work groove, and they are still down there punching a time clock?

Terrible Tilly

What self-respecting ghost wouldn't want to inhabit a lighthouse? With their stormy nights and foggy days, the tall towers on remote rock almost scream out for a supernatural tenant. At the Tillamook Lighthouse, no one seems in the least bit surprised when windows open and shut by themselves, floors creak and heavy sighs hang in the air. Then there's the long spiral staircase winding up to the light.

In his book, *Tillamook Light*, lightkeeper-turned-author James Gibbs writes that it's a startling experience to stand on the spiral staircase and feel the moist breeze blow by. It's like being brushed by a wet blanket.

Tillamook Rock must be one of the most inhospitable places on this earth. A chunk of wave-battered black basalt, it sits one and a half miles from the restless waters of the Pacific. In 1878, it was deemed the best place to build a "first-class lighthouse and steam fog signal" to protect approaching mariners. The only other option was nearby Tillamook Head, 20 miles south of the Columbia River mouth. In spite of its towering location over the ocean, a sheer face made it an impractical choice (not to mention that it was often completely shrouded in dense fog). So the lonely and less lofty outcropping of Tillamook Rock became the chosen site.

Native Americans said the rock was cursed—haunted by evil spirits that caused accidents and boat wrecks. Even before construction began, death plagued the site. One of the first surveyors on the rock—a master mason from Portland—slipped on the slippery rock while trying to get out of his boat. He was sucked into an icy whirlpool and his body was never recovered.

Construction persisted against incalculable odds. It was a major engineering feat, even by today's standards. Crews lived and worked in wretched conditions, lashed by wind and rain, huddled at night in tents as waves washed over the rock. The first challenge was to create a level surface on which the lighthouse could stand. That meant blasting more than 4,600 cubic yards of stubborn stone off the top of the rock. With that accomplished, workers could erect the brick and sandstone dwelling. The lighthouse went into service in January 1881. For the next 77 years, it did its duty faithfully until it was closed and replaced by a radar system. "Terrible Tilly," as it was called after it was abandoned, also picked up a few ghosts.

James Gibbs wrote about his experiences when he was stationed as keeper of the lighthouse from 1945 to 1946. He heard ghostly moans and saw a phantom ship that clipped the rock and lost its rudder. Although he and his fellow lightkeepers sighted the rudder later, they were never able to retrieve it. Others have heard the sound of someone moaning in pain on the second floor of the tower when there was no one else in the building.

Not surprisingly, Tillamook Rock assumed an even stranger identity after it was retired as a navigational aid. In 1980, it became a columbarium where the eccentric could have their ashes interred after death. It would seem safe to say that the chances of this lighthouse being haunted may have subsequently increased a fair bit, what with so many dead folks resting in its catacombs.

Yet the owner, Mimi Morissette, says as far as she knows there are no active ghosts at the lighthouse now. The rock is a private facility and the lighthouse has been completely gutted and sealed to store the remains of those who chose a resting place overlooking the ocean. It's also become something of a wildlife sanctuary. Sea lions, pelicans and murres have returned in abundance. According to Mimi, "It's one of the few places where man and animal peacefully exist side by side."

The Bandage Man

Among malevolent inhuman spirits—i.e., evil spirits that harass human beings, causing all manner of discomfort and distress—the phantom mummy known as the Bandage Man is one horrific creature. At night it lurks on the short stretch of road from Highway 101 to Cannon Beach where it waits for unsuspecting victims and jumps onto the back of their vehicles. The ghost takes the form of a blood-covered man who stinks of rotting flesh and is completely covered in oozing bandages.

Some attacks have been blamed directly on the mummy, because bits of stinking bandages are found at the scene. Locals say it has been known to eat dogs and has murdered some people, although there is no evidence to support that claim.

The Bandage Man is decidedly bad press for a place that counts tourism as its major industry. Cannon Beach is located in the three blocks between the highway and the Pacific Ocean in Clatsop County on the northern Oregon coast. The city was named after a small iron cannon that came ashore in 1846 from a shipwrecked U.S. Navy survey schooner, the *Shark*. It holds kite festivals and sand castle competitions as a way of attracting tourists to the area. The beach itself extends for about four miles along the Pacific Ocean coast. With a tiny population of just over 1500 people, it doesn't take long for stories—especially creepy ghost stories—to get around.

Where the Bandage Man came from is up for debate. One account suggests it is the vengeful spirit of a logger who was cut to pieces in a nearby sawmill. In his book *Oregon's Ghosts and Monsters*, Mike Helm interviews a local who believes the man was killed in a coastal landslide and returned a few days later to exact revenge for his untimely death.

So if you're out for a drive in the area on a stormy night, try to avoid the creepy stretch of Highway 101.

Ghosts of Rhododendron Village

On the west side of Mount Hood, the Cascade Geographic Society is restoring a cluster of buildings that were formerly part of an old logging camp. The 18-acre site will be used for a living history program called the Oregon Country Settlement. Apparitions of pioneers are routinely seen in different buildings. Some have even been caught on camera.

Three segments of the Oregon Trail cross through the site, including the Barlow Trail, which went over Mount Hood. Immigrants and settlers traveled west by wagon in 1845. There are also a number of gravesites on the land, some Native American and some pioneer. Without a doubt, these are the source of some of the ghostly activity that has been recorded recently.

Michael P. Jones heads up the society that bought the land. He is captivated by the rich history of the region and is sure that the site's spirits are pleased at the restoration work. "What I find is that when you start restoring something, they like it," he notes. "Maybe that is why they are letting their presence be known."

Three original buildings from the old logging camp are slowly being renovated—the bunkhouse, the mess hall and the camp owner's house. There were once 12 buildings, but the majority either burned down or collapsed under the strain of many harsh winters. A few newer buildings have been built to replicate the 1890s-style lumber camp. All of them are haunted.

It started with the strange noises. A thump. A bang. A creaking floor. Jones says the staff and volunteers initially attributed the recurring noises to field mice or shifting floorboards. At first, the buildings were mainly used for storage. "But as we restored the buildings to use for displaying artifacts, the noises increased," says Jones.

To keep the project costs under control, much of the work is done by volunteers. Jones tells me that one worker got more than he bargained for when he agreed to stay overnight in the bunkhouse. "I showed up early and he said, 'I had a terrible night,' " Jones explains. "He'd been kept awake all night by loud banging on the walls, ceiling, floor and roof. He was really upset. And I'm wondering what is going on with him."

Not long afterward, a group of seven or eight volunteers also stayed overnight. The next morning, all of them had stories of doors opening and closing and lights turning on and off by themselves. They slept on air mattresses laid out on the floor and reported feeling the floor shake. Jones explains that the building has foundation problems, "so when someone walks in the room, you can feel it."

The group decided to stay, and the next night some of the volunteers got out their cameras. What they photographed shocked them even more. Caught on film were orbs—"crazy lights," in Michael Jones' words. They also tried to get some

Gravesites, both Indian and pioneer, are the source of paranormal activity at this old logging camp near Mount Hood.

of the light activity on video, but something would turn the camera off while they were shooting.

The experience shook up some people. But not Jones. "I'm thinking this is getting interesting," he says. "We're not just hearing things any more." The noises increased to the point where, even during day, people heard thumps. Or they would jump at the sound of something breaking, such as the sound of a vase smashing on the floor. Jones says, given the valuable historic relics kept at the site, they would rush to check it out. No one would be there, and nothing would be out of place.

The building with the most noises is the lumber camp's old mess hall. Essentially one big room, it also has bedrooms at the east and west ends. People have noticed that at about 4 AM the door to the west-end bedroom will open. No one appears, but someone is heard walking across the creaking floor into the kitchen. The belief is that the ghostly cook is locked into his routine of rising early to get ready for breakfast.

The spirits that inhabit the site are becoming more visible. In spring 2001, some workers found two separate rock-covered graves outside the old mess. One was for a pioneer and the other was for a Native American. Aware that the graves were a rare historical find, the volunteers photographed them. They didn't realize they were capturing more than just a few rocks and trees on film. When the pictures came back, the same orbs as seen in the bunkhouse pictures appeared beside the graves. Michael Jones explains that, right around both graves, it looks like there is fog on the photos. "There was no other fog anywhere else," he adds.

"The craziest photo was from October [2001]," says Jones. Someone took a picture of the beautiful old organ in the old mess hall. When the film was developed, the picture contained the surprising image of a pioneer woman in a dark dress reflected in the mirror of the organ above the keyboard. "There is a woman's face," claims Jones. He says the ghost is so clearly visible in the photo that people who previously disputed the source of the noises have abandoned their skepticism.

Michael Jones is not surprised by the ghostly cast of characters that populates the property he oversees. Many immigrant pioneers traveling the Oregon Trail died here. Not far from the Cascade Geographic Society property is the site of the trail's most gruesome accidents—Big Laurel Hill. The formidable rocky hill was so steep that people and wagons had to be lowered by ropes. Dozens of tragedies took place when the ropes would break. The village of Rhododendron, where the historic site is located, was where surviving settlers camped and nursed their wounds before continuing on the grueling trek. The pioneers would bury their dead at their campsites so that they could find them again more easily. They would return later to put up a proper burial marker or to relocate remains to a cemetery nearer to their final destination.

Even the new replica buildings that the society built have stories associated with them. Jones theorizes that the spirits feel comfortable in the copies because they look familiar. It helps that they are filled with artifacts from the period—furniture, old tools and artwork.

Added to the growing body of photographic and oral evidence are Michael's own firsthand experiences of the supernatural. Once, he was out in the trading post, which will one day be filled with old logging tools for display. "I was standing there and I could feel something walk towards me. The floor was bouncing," he recalls.

Nearby in the village of Welches, the Cascade Geographic Society has an interpretive center with its own ghost stories. It may have something to do with the pioneer viewing casket that they have on display. The rare, child-sized antique was on sale in a Washington coast antique store when it was "rescued." The viewing casket is made of wicker and lined with satin. Caskets like it were rented for the funeral service, after which the body would be transferred to a traditional pine box for burial. Jones says, "We put it in one of our showcases, and ever since the night we brought it there, people have claimed they could see the ghost of a young girl in pioneer dress playing in the great hall. The witnesses see her through a window at night, but when they try to get in, the door is locked."

The Phantom Bugler

Around Forest Grove in Washington County, a nasty spirit walks the woods. He has been blamed for the deaths of several hikers.

It is the ghost of an old bugler—an imposing man and talented hunter who was hired by the government to track down lawbreakers more than 70 years ago. He used to live in a cabin deep in the woods. While he was alive, the bugler always carried an oversize horn, slung over his shoulder on a strap. He played it as he roamed through the woods. Once, during a cougar attack, it served as a handy weapon.

As the lore goes, the bugler bludgeoned the animal to death just in time to save his own life. He was seriously cut up in the attack and badly scarred. The locals say it turned him crazy. After the assault, legend has it that he wandered through the forest looking for victims to attack. If he encountered some unlucky person, he would beat him or her to death with the bugle.

The bugler died some time ago. But every now and then a body will be found with its head split open, possibly from a blow by an oversized bugle. This story appeals to thrill-seekers who like the idea of a terrifying night in the woods. In other words, it's very "Blair Witch."

The Klamath Lady

Although the legend of the Klamath Lady is well known around the coastal town of Siletz, there are differing interpretations of how she came to be. The result is the same, though, and can make for a creepy drive along the Siletz River on a stormy night.

No date is attached to the story, but it is said that many years back a woman of the Klamath Indian band was crossing the Siletz River on the old bridge with her husband and her baby. Depending on which version you hear, she and her baby were either pushed in the river after a vicious fight with her husband or she jumped in with her child to follow her husband who had fallen in and drowned. No one ever found the bodies of the woman or baby.

People who live in the area believe she haunts the road that runs next to where she died. On blustery evenings, a gray-cloaked figure is seen wandering on the grade by the river carrying a bundle the size of a baby. Legend has it that if you stop to give the person a lift, she will sit in the back of the vehicle and not allow her face to be seen. If you don't look at her, she disappears once the car goes past the grade. Those who choose not to stop and offer a ride are doomed to crash. This is one occasion when it may pay to pick up a lone woman walking out in the rain.

Rue, the Ghost of Heceta Head

On the rocky promontory of Oregon's coast, just north of Florence, a lighthouse beacon flashes its warning to all who sail past. For more than a hundred years, sailors have been spared from crashing on the craggy coast by the piercing beam of light at Heceta Head. But people rarely talk about the site's role in keeping mariners safe. Most tongues wag about the gray-sheathed ghost, Rue.

Just a few feet farther down the cliff stands the lighthouse keeper's gleaming three-story house. It looks much as it did a century ago when first erected as a home for the caretakers of Heceta Head. According to lighthouse lore, it is inhabited by the spirit of a woman who lived there in the early 1900s. One day, her toddler wandered outdoors and fell off the cliffs into the sea. Many years later, the grief-stricken mother died of old age, having always longed for her child's return. Another version of the legend suggests the child drowned after falling into the cistern and the body is buried somewhere in the overgrown brambles between the house and the lighthouse. Some former custodians say the woman's spirit remains simply out of a deep love for her home. Her name, Rue, apparently surfaced one year during a Ouija board session.

Certainly one of Oregon's most well-known ghosts, Rue makes her presence known in subtle ways. As one caretaker noted, she doesn't fling bloody hatchets about. Instead, the gray lady of Heceta House moves tools, flicks on lights, opens windows and closes curtains.

The lighthouse opened in 1894. The keepers operated it around the clock, tending to a five-wick coal oil lamp and an eight-panel lens with 640 prisms. Passing ships could see the

A benevolent spirit named Rue still looks after the lightkeeper's house at Heceta Head.

light 20 miles from shore. The light still reaches as far, but the lighthouse was automated in 1963.

The adjacent house was built as a duplex for the two assistant lighthouse keepers and their families. The head keeper lived next door in a similar house that was torn down in 1940. Over the years, the old home passed over to the U.S. Forest Service, which leases it to Lane Community College for classes and seminars.

Reports of Rue's handiwork date back several decades. One of the most famous incidents happened while caretakers Harry and Anne Tammen lived in the home in the mid-1970s. At first, the couple blamed the noises in the house on the gale force winds that often buffet the coast. They even put out rat poison in the attic in case the sounds had an organic source. The poison was mysteriously replaced with a single silk stocking. In other instances, cupboard doors, securely shut at night, were open the next morning. The noises and goings-on continued until one day when a workman came face to face with the home's otherworldly mistress.

Jim Alexander and his son Dave had been contracted to repair the upper story. Unexplained happenings began right away. Tools disappeared, only to reappear in different parts of the house. Padlocks mysteriously opened. Sandpaper vanished so often they ran out. They tried to offer up logical explanations until the tools and sandpaper would disappear and reappear in the same spot.

One day, Jim was working in the attic, which he reached by a ladder through a trapdoor. As he was cleaning a glass window overlooking the ocean, he saw strange reflections of what looked like someone standing behind him. It was a bright morning and sunlight streamed into the attic. When he turned around, he says, "I saw this elderly lady with a long gown and long gray hair watching me." The woman wore an 1890s-style gown. She floated across the attic between him and the trapdoor. Jim recalled her appearance in several interviews after the event. The apparition was old and wrinkled, but had a slim, youthful body. Her long hair and gown flowed behind her as she stood there, saying nothing. Terrified, the carpenter dove through the trapdoor and ran from the house, never to return. The ghost reappeared in his dreams for the next four nights. Each time she asked him to return and continue his repair work.

It took Jim a long time to summon the courage to return to the job. He refused to enter the attic, so he would climb to the second story from outside the house. While he was working, Jim accidentally broke an attic window with a hammer. He fixed it from the outside, leaving the broken glass where it fell on the attic floor.

Sometime later, the Tammens woke to hear a scratching noise coming from the attic, like a broom sweeping. Harry climbed up and found a pile of glass shards, remnants of the broken window, carefully swept into a neat, circular pile. He didn't even know that the window had been broken. Maybe Rue was worried that one of the Tammens would walk in and be injured by the broken glass? Or perhaps she is a barefoot ghost who didn't like the idea of stepping on the dangerous shards?

Since then, most of the custodians have collected stories about Rue. The Tammens, who started out as skeptics, say they saw her a number of times, usually while they were doing domestic chores. However, during a card party one night Rue obviously wanted some attention. The Tammens and two guests were scared by what they described as a high-pitched scream.

Others besides the Tammens have sensed a supernatural presence in the house. Two students who were visiting Heceta House reported seeing something gray float up the porch steps. They described what they saw as long and flowing, almost like a puff of smoke.

In the early 1990s, Duncan and Carolyn Stockton heard odd noises, like a cough in the hallway outside their bedroom. They assumed it was Rue when they heard the crunch of gravel on the path behind them or a click on the stairs as if she was following. Their strangest and most shocking incident involved a grease fire in the kitchen. Unable to put out the ceiling high flames, Carolyn called the local fire department. She had to meet them in the lane to open the gate, but by the time the firefighters entered the kitchen, the fire was out. And to everyone's surprise, there were no signs of scorching or flame or even much smoke. In the department's official report, it was noted that the fire was extinguished "by persons unknown."

Ten years later, Mike and Carol Korgan were running the house as a small inn. They often noticed the scent of fresh lavender despite an absence of fresh flowers. One newlywed couple claims to have returned from a stroll to find their room had been tidied. Rue, it seems, can't bear a mess.

In *Ghosts of the West Coast,* Ted Wood cites an example of another couple that had a startling wake-up call while staying at the inn for their 25th anniversary. The woman woke at 4 AM to hear an odd electrical buzz near her head. She didn't open her eyes out of fear, but she could sense light through her eyelids. She felt something gently touch her hand. As the buzzing moved away, she opened her eyes to see a glowing ball of red light pass through the door. The woman wrote the experience off as a dream, until her husband asked her the next day if she had seen the strange glow over their bed.

As recently as January 2002, Nancy Collister, an avid lighthouse enthusiast, wrote a column for *Oregon Coast* about a mysterious encounter on a dark December night. Nancy and her golden retriever, Tanner, visited the lighthouse on a Friday night. The area was deserted. They walked past the house and on toward the lighthouse, using a flashlight to illuminate the trail. When they got to the edge of the cliff near the lighthouse, Nancy's dog refused to go any farther. The trembling animal sniffed in the direction of the fenced-off area on the cliff. Nancy says she could just make out the shape of a person wearing a long, dark coat peering out over the ocean. She was prepared to move closer to meet the person, but Tanner's terror convinced her it might not be a good idea. They both bolted for Nancy's truck and drove off. To this day, Nancy wonders if she witnessed the ghostly mother in a dark cloak looking out to sea, as other visitors have reported.

Like the continual crash of the surf below, Rue is a persistent yet generally pleasant presence at Heceta Head. She makes sure her home is well cared for.

2

Haunted
Hotels

The Geiser Grand Hotel

Women vanish into walls. China moves by itself. Invisible presences laugh and drink into the wee hours at the Geiser Grand Hotel. Is it haunted? The owners say they haven't drawn any firm conclusions, but they believe the spirits of the gold rush are alive within the hotel's opulent walls.

The gold mining boom brought a lot of money to Baker City. Dreamers and schemers mixed with politicians, cattle barons and timber magnates. The Geiser family saw an opportunity to bring these groups together under one roof, so they built the stunning Geiser Grand Hotel in 1889. Opened the same year as New York's Waldorf Astoria, it was a place of stunning excess where white-gloved waiters served fresh Maine lobster and turtle soup in rooms lit with more than 100 crystal chandeliers. Guests today experience the magnificence of a bygone era the moment they enter the lobby. If they stay for any length of time, they might also meet some of the guests from times past. As in many century-old hotels, traces of energy from parties that shook the walls remain at the Geiser Grand.

Owners Barbara and Dwight Sidway maintain the hotel according to Czech designer John Benes' original intentions. The Geiser family spared no expense in creating a showcase for the wealth they had acquired from the Bonanza and other gold mines in the region. It was one of the first hotels in Oregon to offer electricity, and it boasted the third elevator west of the Mississippi River. With its stained glass ceiling, mahogany millwork, Romanesque jambs and a 200-foot corner cupola, the house is like a museum. Ten-foot high windows allow for breathtaking views of the mountains that surround Baker City.

The lavish Geiser Grand Hotel in Baker City, c. 1900

It's hard to imagine the historic building sliding into decay, but over the years financial hardship took its toll. The building was used as a brothel, a casino and a veteran's hospital before closing in 1968. By then it had fallen into serious disrepair. The Sidways bought the hotel in 1993. It reopened in 1997 after nearly four years and $6 million worth of painstaking restoration. All the activity seems to have disturbed some of the ghostly residents.

Barbara Sidway says the first hints of spirits in the hotel came from the work crews. Toward the end of the renovation project, with a deadline to open looming, they ran three shifts. "I know it's cliché, but the guys working the midnight shift had the experiences," she tells me. Tools and equipment moved after being set down. Workers heard voices of people laughing and talking when no one else was in the building.

"The most chilling story was just before the hotel reopened," recalls Barbara. "A trusted long-term employee who still works for us was walking down a corridor and saw someone walking ahead of him. He followed the person into a room, but when he walked through the door no one was there, just cold air. He was stunned, completely dumbfounded."

The locus of peculiar activity seems to be in the Cupola Suite, which is right under the clock tower. During the final stages of the renovation, Barbara had set up a workshop in the suite for women who were working with the textiles, sewing things such as curtains. The lock to the room was a constant source of irritation because it never seemed to work properly. A newer magnetic lock, it would demagnetize itself or be fussy. A worker was reinstalling the lock for at least the third time when one of the women who worked in the room said to Barbara, "I don't know why you are trying to fix that. The ghosts are never going to let you have this room." The woman was quite certain that spirits lived in the room. Barbara says she didn't think much of it at the time. But those words came back to haunt her—literally.

"The next event that was quite astonishing happened shortly after the hotel opened for business," says Barbara. "The Cupola Suite had not been occupied, but a maid went to do a routine check while on her rounds. When she opened the door, she was shocked to see everything in the room had been tossed upside down. It was completely topsy-turvy. The windows are ten feet high, and the long curtains were all twisted and looped. The covers were pulled off the bed, the pillows had been tossed everywhere."

Barbara realizes it is possible that someone somehow got a key and pulled a prank by making it look like a ghost had been there. "Or did the spirits give us a sign that they don't want people there? I don't know," she says. "It just poses the questions. There are no answers."

Once the ghost stories started surfacing, the media began to investigate the veracity of the tales. Barbara says one reporter from *Newsweek* got closer to the truth than she expected. The reporter stayed in the Cupola Suite and she told Barbara the next morning over breakfast that a female ghost had come into the bedroom and sat down on the bed next to her. Although the reporter didn't claim to see an apparition, she said she smelled perfume and sensed the ghost's presence.

The other stories take place mainly in the hotel's public areas, from the Bonanza Room downstairs to the grand staircase and the kitchen. Barbara's opinion is that her ghosts are still enjoying the rollicking good times of the gold mining boom years. "I get a sense that all of the spirits date to the 1920s and earlier. It seems there are a bunch of partying ghosts." That would explain the loud parties with no visible guests.

One night Barbara and Dwight were sleeping in the hotel for the first time, up on the second floor. The rooms had opened in stages, and the third floor had not yet opened to the public. "It was after midnight and I could hear music, the tinkle of glasses and lots of voices, at least a dozen or so. I thought, *What's going on?* It was the middle of the week, after hours." Dwight called down to see why the bar was open so late, but it was closed and no one answered. Barbara, now wide awake, put her ear to the wall to determine from which part of the hotel the noise emanated. The sounds were clearly audible.

"Dwight heard it too, so he went out and investigated," says Barbara. He returned to say the disturbance was coming from the third floor. He guessed that a group had sneaked up there and broken into a room for their after-hours celebration. Dwight went up to confront the people, but when he reached the third floor the sound stopped. He hunted through the rooms to no avail. No one was there. Dwight checked through the hotel, and even looked in the street, but he didn't find a party.

The Sidways didn't think of it again, until they were told by old timers in the town that such unseen parties were regular occurrences more than 60 years ago. One bartender who worked in the hotel in the 1940s was surprised that Barbara didn't know about the stories. The parties still go on even now, and many of the sounds originate from the Bonanza Room in the northeast corner of the hotel. It serves as a meeting room these days, but it used to host high-stakes poker games. On several occasions, bartenders have reported hearing a party at closing time. They naturally check to see who is still lingering in the hotel, but each time they find the room empty.

In the kitchen, a prankster spirit moves glasses and china. Some people think it may be the energy of a chef who met a tragic end in a horrible dumbwaiter accident some 80 years ago. Although there are no apparitions, something definitely shifts things about. One kitchen employee watched as a case of glasses lifted up off a counter in a storage room, moved through the air and then fell to the floor, as if an unseen person carrying it decided to just let it drop. A Japanese documentary crew claims they caught paranormal activity on camera when they were filming in the kitchen. Apparently, their camera recorded a glass moving by itself.

Another prankster lives in the bar. Again, when most people have gone home, the bartenders will feel a presence. Then the bar tap to the draft beer pulls down by itself.

There are also a few visible ghosts that live in the Geiser Grand. The "Lady in Blue," for example, regularly walks up and down the grand staircase. Barbara hasn't seen the ghost herself, but others have described the female apparition many times. "It's a Gibson girl wearing a long, lavender dress. She walks up the staircase and disappears into the wall."

Then there are the flapper-style party girls who hang out on the second floor balustrade balcony. On two separate occasions, psychics came to Barbara to tell her they could see several women leaning over the balcony watching the people below. The women are floating there, without solid legs or feet, enjoying all the activity.

Some hotel guests report things that may or may not be connected to the hotel's ghosts. "There's the famous carrot cake incident," laughs Barbara. "One guest called down to say that in the middle of the night, a ghost ate the cake they had in the room." Another guest told the front desk that he awoke to the sound of water running. For some reason, the shower was running though no one was in the bathroom. Barbara's suspicion is that the power of suggestion may be behind most of the things that happen in the guest's rooms, but it's difficult to be certain.

Renovations to the Geiser Grand seem to have awakened ghosts of a bygone era.

As for her take on the various spirits, Barbara says that after 20 years doing historic restorations, she has learned to keep an open mind. She and Dwight worked on the Biltmore Hotel project in Florida, which had been shuttered for more than 60 years when they got there. "There were quite a few incidents there that are difficult to explain. Having gone through that experience, someone would at least be open to the possibility that ghostly hauntings can occur. You don't have to be a believer, but we've both seen a lot."

Barbara believes the spirit activity happens when buildings have been closed for long periods of time because the entities can roam freely, undetected. Once the building is restored and reopened, the ghosts start bumping into earthbound humans until they either leave or decide to avoid them.

The Mark Antony

A stay at the newly renovated Mark Antony Hotel, now called the Ashland Springs, may offer some extra services that you won't see on the bill—like visits from a ghostly bellman who opens the door without prompting.

It's not the kind of thing the new owners are too keen on publicizing. Doug and Becky Neuman bought the historic but dilapidated building in 1998. According to their website, the couple have undertaken a "basement to parapet remodel" of the hotel. They prefer to focus on the hotel's elegance and grandeur, not its eerie ghosts. Still, they took the tales of ghosts seriously. After investing heavily to restore the landmark, they didn't want any spooky spirits to scare away guests. To this end, they called in the religious leaders of the community and held a ceremony to bless the building and purge its ghosts.

After 75 years, it seems reasonable that "The Mark" might have a few extra spirits on the premises, especially since some Native Americans claim that the hotel sits on an Indian burial ground. Most of the hauntings, however, appear modern in nature, involving former guests who float around the mezzanine level.

The nine-story building opened in 1925 as the Lithia Springs Hotel. The tallest structure between Portland and San Francisco, the 100-room hotel offered a luxurious retreat for travelers who came either to hear the Chautauqua lectures or to bathe in the famous Lithia Springs water, which was reputed to be good for one's health. Tourism was relatively new to the Rogue Valley in the 1920s but the Lithia Springs Hotel was ear-marked by promoters as the business that could compete with the fashionable hotels back east. When it opened on July 1, 1925, 500 guests from Oregon and northern California enjoyed a sumptuous dinner that was meant to initiate an era of affluence and success. Unfortunately, the glory days were short-lived.

Two years after the hotel opened, direct passenger train service to Ashland was cancelled. That cut back on visits by the wealthy clientele. They stopped coming and the hotel began to struggle. Various owners tried to prop up the failing business, but they couldn't overcome a string of economic downturns. Ultimately, there was more hardship than happiness at the Lithia Springs. In 1960, it was transformed into the Mark Antony and given an English Tudor theme to tie into the growing popularity of the Shakespeare festival. That worked for a while, but it closed again in 1997, emptied of furniture and left to decay until nearly beyond salvage.

That's where the Neumans come in. They have restored the hotel to its original majesty, creating the 70-room Ashland Springs Hotel. The building has been completely refurbished; no detail was overlooked—including the spooks. The Neumans knew of the ghost stories when they bought the hotel, having heard that one room in particular seemed to be haunted. Room 517 on the fifth floor was said to have a presence that could be felt by guests. There were also stories that the ghost of a boy haunted one of the rooms. He is remembered for opening the door of one particular room three nights in a row, at the same time each night. Speculation is that he was either a guest or a former bellboy, though no one knows for sure. In addition, guests and employees had reported seeing shadowy figures lurking about the hotel mezzanine at night.

The general manager explained that when the hotel opened, all the local religious leaders were invited to perform a ceremonial blessing. It required an entire morning. Afterward, there was a group blessing in the lobby. And that seems to have had the desired effect. Since then, there have been "a couple of incidents" that the general manager chose not to reveal. He says that now that the hotel has been given a new lease on life, the management prefers to focus on the future and let the spirits of the past rest in peace.

Oar House Bed and Breakfast

In the 1900s, the Bradshaw Boarding House was used by itinerant dock workers and sailors who stayed in Newport. In the 1920s, the three-story house operated as a bordello. Its present incarnation, the Oar House, is a charming five-room bed and breakfast. But be prepared—there may be some non-paying ghostly guests.

Built from the timbers of shipwrecks scavenged from the beaches, the original boarding house evolved as materials washed up on shore. More wood meant more rooms. This explains idiosyncrasies of construction that offer everything from a huge ocean-view room to a steep, irregular staircase that leads to the crow's nest—a third-floor attic perfect for the vertically challenged.

Local lore has it that a woman came to meet her fiancé in the 1930s when the house was still a brothel. She found work there as a maid while she waited patiently for her love to arrive. As months passed, she eventually realized her fiancé was not coming to get her. The dejected woman is said to have thrown herself out of a third-floor window to her death on the ground below.

The current innkeeper, Jan LeBrun, says the previous owner told her he had encountered the woman's ghost. The spirit apparently lay down to have a nap with him one afternoon. He was waiting for his wife with his back to the door. He heard someone cross the room and felt the bed move. When he rolled over to speak to his wife, no one was there.

Jan, however, has not seen a ghost since she bought the inn in 1992. As she puts it, "I have had no personal encounters with a ghost. I tend not to believe in ghosts. I think the propensity to believe in them affects one's encounters."

Still, a couple of things are hard to explain. Sometimes guests complain that the attic room overheats for no apparent reason. And a guest at her daughter's wedding asked if the third-floor room was haunted after spending a few sleepless nights in it. "And I had one guest sitting in a room on the main floor who said he felt a presence," says Jan, who admits she is not keen on promoting the paranormal aspect of the property.

David Bradshaw laughed when I contacted him about ghosts in the house. His grandfather and great-grandfather built the boarding house, and David has lived in Newport all his life. In all his 52 years, he has never heard of any otherworldly beings living there. Oddly enough, though, he did say that his grandfather, Harrison Wright Bradshaw, admitted to "haunting" the nearby Yaquina Bay Lighthouse as a child (the structure was supposed to be haunted by the spirit of a captain's daughter). Bradshaw would lie on the floor moaning and groaning to scare people into thinking there really was a ghost. It's possible that many of the local spirits are nothing other than the playful souls of young people who have lived in Newport over the years.

The Ghostly Stagecoach

The northbound stagecoach rolls in at 11 AM every day. The passengers laugh and disembark. But these visitors are invisible, and the Galesville Hotel, where the stage stops, burned down more than 70 years ago.

Zedekiah Stone, a territorial colonel, operated the six-horse stagecoaches that made the daily journey through the Sexton and Siskiyou Mountains. The old Galesville Hotel in Douglas County was an important stop on the route. In the late 1800s, hotel owner Dan Levens ran a livery barn that sheltered up to 90 horses. Tales of intrigue at the stagecoach station date back more than 130 years. In 1868, an employee robbed the Levens station of $9000 worth of gold dust and coin. Fire destroyed the Galesville Hotel in 1931. Eventually, a farmhouse was constructed on the hotel foundations. Out in the yard, the giant maples planted by Dan Levens still show scars from the fire.

An article printed in the Roseburg newspaper in 1973 contained an account from Charlie and Peggy Van Vlake that suggested someone was still riding the stage out of Rogue River.

The Van Vlakes told reporter Lavola Bakken that soon after they moved into the house, they heard squealing sounds and the laughter of children outside. At first they thought they were hearing their own grandchildren arriving. Even their two Siamese cats heard the noise and ran for cover, avoiding children as only Siamese cats can. When the couple went to see who was in the driveway, they saw nothing; only the low of their grazing cattle greeted them. They knew a car couldn't come into their long drive and turn around without being seen. At first, they had no explanation. But when they learned the history of the site, they realized that what they had heard was likely the phantom sounds of a ghostly coach arriving.

Such a conclusion may seem odd because many definitions describe a ghost as the visible, or partially visible, manifestation of a deceased human or animal. But another explanation for a ghost is that it's a kind of recording, similar to an audio or video tape. In this sense, a ghost is really just the residual energy of a person, animal or even an inanimate object (such as a stagecoach). There is no life force left; the ghost is caught in a time loop and continuously replays the same scene. Usually, if a person or thing has performed a repetitious act for a long period of time, he or she or it will leave a psychic impression or groove in that area. This groove may stay in the area long after the person or thing who created it has moved on or died. This psychic groove is said to be very vivid when it is first encountered. The apparition appears or sounds real. Over time, the groove, or ghost, may weaken, but can be recharged under the right circumstances. In this case, perhaps the daily stagecoach left a groove that ran right through the Van Vlake home.

Hearing the rattle of the stagecoach was one thing, but the leaping wine bottle was altogether different. Charlie told the reporter that they watched as an empty wine bottle jumped out of the garbage can it was in. Then it rolled across the floor, as if pushed by an unseen hand or foot. Not an easy thing to do, given the bottle's square shape. Charlie noted that he didn't think the alcohol had any impact on what they saw.

Peggy had a more personal encounter with something in the house while her daughter was visiting from Georgia.

They were preparing to paint the living room when they both heard two women talking. They couldn't make out what the women were saying, but the two of them agreed someone was there. It was summer and doors were open to allow air to move. Had their neighbors come over for an unannounced visit? Voices in rural areas carry much farther than in a noisy city, and it seemed likely that they were heard people talking as they walked up the lane. Maybe their voices were carried into the house by summer breezes. But no one was outside. The only possibility was that there were people in the house. They looked through all the rooms but saw no one, and yet they heard the voices of two women continue to chat as though they were busy visiting.

At other times, Charlie and Peggy also heard sounds coming from upstairs. They said it sounded like someone reading or leafing through a magazine. Again, when they ventured up to see what had made the noise, they couldn't find anything or anyone. Perhaps the ghosts were leafing through a book or magazine while they waited patiently for the next stagecoach to arrive.

In her book, *The Mysterious Doom*, Jessica Salmonson includes an account from the grandson of a Levens descendent who lived on the farm before the Van Vlakes. Although he was an old man when he recounted his tale, his memories were as vivid as if they had just happened. This is hardly surprising when you hear what he lived through.

As a young man, he had also heard the sound of the stagecoach arriving each morning while visiting his grandparents at the farm. But one day he looked out the window and was shocked to see a six-horse stagecoach coming down the road toward the house. Not aware of any historic festivals in the area, he ran to ask his grandfather about the coach. His grandfather told him not to worry about it because the coach would be gone already. Seems the old man took the ghostly stage in stride.

The stagecoach sighting alerted the grandson to other strange events in the house. He saw a comb leap from an end table without any visible cause. But that would seem insignificant in comparison to his terrifying journey home one day.

Bored from too many days on the farm, the young man went into Galesville for a few drinks. He overindulged and passed out in the bar. Embarrassed to have slept in the tavern all night, he raced home the next day in his grandparents' Ford. About four miles from the farm, a tire blew and he careened into the ditch. Dazed, he got out and started walking along the road toward the farm. As he made his way in the summer heat, the rattle of the stagecoach came from behind. To the young man's surprise, the driver halted the stage and asked him if he needed a ride. Although he knew the coach was being driven by a ghost, he still agreed to accept the lift.

The door to the stagecoach opened by itself. That might have been enough to stop some people, but he got in anyway. Inside the carriage, he saw a woman in Victorian dress holding a fan to her face and two men with silk hats in their laps. The stage began to move. The man realized with a start that he couldn't hear the sound of the horses from inside. He didn't think he was still drunk, so he asked his traveling companions where they were from. The woman lowered her fan and revealed a face without flesh. The two men's faces had also turned into skulls. Terrified, he threw open the carriage door, but outside there was nothing but gray mist. As the ghosts reached out to touch him, he leapt out of the moving stagecoach.

Falling into the gray mist, the man says he saw a face appear. At first he thought it was his grandfather, but then realized it was an elderly Native American who just looked like his grandfather. He grabbed the young man's arm and yanked him hard. The next thing he knew, he was lying by the side of the road at the farmhouse. His grandparents rushed to help him, asking what had happened. He never told them. All he could say was that the car had a flat tire and that he'd driven into the ditch. His grandparents died without ever knowing of the experience. But he was a changed man, believing for certain that there are things that exist beyond what we see on this plane.

Hot Lake Resort

Built in in the 1880s, Hot Lake Resort was known as "The Mayo Clinic of the West." It was extremely popular for the curative powers of its thermal hot springs. In fact, the construction of the Hot Lake Hotel near La Grande marked the first time in U.S. history that the energy from geothermal springs was used on a large scale. Hundreds of visitors came from around the world to experience the waters, including the famous Mayo Brothers who were friends of Dr. Phy, the administrator.

People arrived daily by train to heal and restore themselves in the 205-degree waters, aided by sumptuous cuisine and the stunning natural beauty of the scenic Grande Ronde valley. According to an article dated November 6, 1949, in the *Spokesman Review,* the hotel employed 175 staff at its peak and served 2000 to 3000 meals every day. Fire destroyed a large portion of the elegant gabled building in 1934, and the resort never fully recovered. It eventually changed hands, becoming first a convalescent hospital, then a nursing home and finally a restaurant and hotel before it closed permanently to the public. It slid into decline, becoming a dilapidated wreck.

But Hot Lake Resort still attracts the attention of passersby, perhaps out of curiosity about the ghosts that are said to haunt what remains of the once-sprawling complex. Now that the property and the huge brick building are privately owned (with "No Trespassing" signs everywhere), visits might not be beneficial to one's health. In the years when the resort functioned as a single floor hotel and restaurant, however, there were many accounts of ghostly goings-on.

During the 1970s, Dave and Donna Pattee operated a restaurant and hotel on the first floor. They soon discovered their business had a bizarre feature. Overnight guests reported hearing strange sounds from the empty upper floors including piano playing and—more disturbing—horrible screams. Donna Pattee says her mother lived on the first floor for a while. She insisted that from her room she could hear people walking the hallways at night when everyone was asleep. "She used to prop a chair up under her door at night."

Other guests reported hearing notes from a piano that sat on the abandoned third floor. Sometimes the playing would last several minutes. The sounds of people laughing and having a party would also waft down to the guests on the main floor. Eventually, the Pattees moved the piano into the dining room. That didn't stop the playing. One evening, when their son was in the room with some friends, the music began even though no one was near the instrument.

Richard Owens, a caretaker who lived on the second floor, wasn't bothered by the music. But he found the screams overhead difficult to bear. His room was directly

Dave and Donna Pattee relate many ghost stories about Hot Lake Resort, once considered "The Mayo Clinic of the West."

underneath the old hospital surgery and he said he regularly heard a woman crying out in agony. Donna said Rick also told her he heard the chairs on the third floor rocking at night.

Whatever prowled about the old resort also liked to move things around. Chairs would be placed in one configuration by Donna only to be rearranged when she would go back. There were three rocking chairs on the upper story that never seemed to need dusting, as if someone was routinely sitting in them. Donna was surprised one time when she found the chairs set up in a neat semicircle. The last time she had checked, they were scattered randomly around the third-floor room.

Richard Owens says he was constantly pushing the piano bench back under the piano when it was on the third floor, despite the fact that no one ever went up there.

The Pattee family moved out in 1977. Now that the resort is privately owned, it's not known if the spirits continue to entertain other phantom guests and roam about the old hallways.

The Welches Roadhouse

An hour east of Portland, at the western base of Mount Hood, is the town of Welches. The Salmon River flows through the historic foothills region, which is now home to some very upscale golf and ski resorts. It also lays claim to a few lingering ghosts that keep the place interesting.

The old Welches Roadhouse on Roberts Avenue is a two-story cedar home with two ghosts. One is believed to be a former female innkeeper who may have died in the house. The other ghost that is often sensed there is a male presence. It may be the ghost of an escaped convict that the innkeeper was hiding there.

Michael Jones, who runs the Cascade Geographic Society and is writing his own book of local ghost stories and folklore, told me about the remarkable history of the roadhouse.

It started with Samuel Welch, the village founder and owner of the first hotel. Welch was an Oregon Trail pioneer who arrived in the area in the 1840s. As he crossed the Blue Mountains and saw the scenic beauty of Mount Hood, Welch knew that Oregon's tallest peak would provide the perfect backdrop for a resort. With that in mind, he worked toward fulfilling his dream. Welch moved up to Mount Hood in 1880 and by 1889 he had enlarged his family home on the west bank of the Salmon River enough to turn it into a hotel. It was called the Big House, and on July 1 the first guests began to arrive.

The roadhouse was built to accommodate the overflow of tourists. The female owner would take in guests when Welch's hotel was full. The two-story home incorporated a few odd construction details, the most obvious being two doors on the upper floor that opened to the outdoors but had no staircase. Unsuspecting guests had to be wary or they would find themselves dropping unceremoniously to the ground floor. The belief is that the doors were built as an escape route in the event of an extreme snowstorm. In those days, it was not unusual for a blizzard to dump several feet of snow, trapping people indoors.

As the story goes, one day there was a jailbreak in Portland and several escapees showed up at the roadhouse looking for a safe place to hide out. The innkeeper and one of the men were attracted to each other and had an affair. When search parties arrived, the couple hid in a secret room on the second floor, which could only be accessed by a ladder.

The tryst did not last. The bandit knew it would be too dangerous to remain when tourist season resumed in summer, so he fled. His broken-hearted lover committed suicide by walking out of one of the second-story doors and falling to her death.

Michael Jones says the other ghosts—and there are several—are those of Native American spirits. The road-house is built on an old campground that was once an Indian fishing site where huckleberries were dried. Many Native Americans are buried there, and some of their spirits haunt the now privately owned home.

Jones has visited the house and tells me, "It is a very eerie place. If you sit in the living room, you can hear somebody walking on the second floor. You know there is no one up there. Then you hear someone stop at the top of the stairs and walk down. You can tell where he is by the creaking of the floors, but no one is there."

Another time, Jones watched as a rocking chair began to move by itself. And children's balls are often seen rolling on the floor by themselves or bouncing down the stairs. The different owners vary widely in their experiences. Jones says some people tell him they hear nothing. When asked if they've encountered anything unusual, others recall a litany of things that have happened.

The Haunted Heathman

Anyone who regularly stays or has worked at Portland's historic Heathman Hotel will hear about room 703 sooner or later. Within the lavish interior of the 75-year-old building, it seems someone chose not to check out.

There are countless accounts, often told to bemused front desk staff, from guests who check in, leave the room for a few hours and return to find a glass of water on the desk. Or a chair moved. Or the television turned on. The guest calls the concierge to report an intrusion, but when the concierge checks the electronic key record it reveals that no one had been in the room since the first guest left. It might be possible to explain this away one or two times, but this has been happening regularly in 703 for years. Chairs change position, towels are used and yet no entry is recorded on the room key.

In 1999, a psychic staying in room 803, one floor above the notorious suite, claimed to see a ghost at the end of her bed. Char Margolis, author of *Questions From Earth, Answers From Heaven*, theorized that someone had jumped to his death and now haunts all the rooms that were passed on the way down. Built in 1927, the sumptuous hotel—complete with an Italian Renaissance façade and lush decor—may have been too lovely to leave.

When I spoke to Marvin at reception, he said he hasn't seen or experienced anything since he joined the hotel in the mid-1980s. But he has heard frequent accounts from both guests and colleagues that convince him some spirit is roaming the area near room 703. Recently, one of the concierges was taking the elevator that operates next to the "03" column of rooms. When she turned to look in the elevator mirror, she saw the reflection of another person. Shocked, she looked behind her to find she was, as when she entered, alone in the car. Marvin has also heard from terrified housekeeping staff members who have seen a male ghost, though it doesn't stick around long enough for them to offer a good description.

Kathleen at the front desk says there have also been odd occurrences in room 702. Lights turn on and off by themselves. It may be a simple electrical problem or perhaps it is the ghost looking to expand its territory.

Many people have reported feeling cold spots or hearing whispered voices in the halls and footsteps descending the hotel's grand staircase. If you ask the old-timers, they'll tell you it's all part of the Heathman experience.

Oregon Caves Lodge

Where better than in the land of Bigfoot to find a ghost that haunts an old lodge built onto the side of a mountain? Deep in the dense forests that are southwestern Oregon's trademark, the Oregon Caves Lodge is rumored to be permanent host to the ghost of a heartbroken newlywed.

The lodge was built in 1927 in response to the swelling number of tourists on their way through the bush to one of Oregon's natural miracles. Deep in the heart of Mount Elijah, local hunter Elijah Davidson stumbled upon a labyrinth of caves back in 1874. Thirty-three years later, the pillars, stalactites and canopies of calcite that line the passageways and dome of the caves inspired the poet Joaquin Miller to name the caverns "The Marble Halls of Oregon." The limestone formations cover 480 acres of horizontal space on several different levels. Many of the incredible shapes resemble marble carvings of objects such as flowers and a pipe organ. One large chamber, which is 250 feet long and 50 feet wide, is filled with what appear to be gray robed figures. It has been appropriately nicknamed the "ghost room." Miller's glamorous prose drew attention to this undiscovered gem and fueled a booming tourist trade.

After the caves received status as a national monument in 1909, the U.S. Forest Service began running official tours. It's only natural that someone would soon erect a place for tourists to stay.

The Oregon Caves Lodge is right across from the entrance to the caves. It's a six-story building designed by architect Gust Lium in 1934. Over the years, little has changed. Hugging the embankment, the ten-sided structure features a double-hearth marble fireplace in the lobby. The 1930s-style coffee shop retains its winding birch and maple counter. And in the dining room, a stream of water diverted from Cave Creek flows through the room. Two small mounds were built as bridges so guests and waiters could cross from one side of the room to the other.

The hotel was an overnight success. Instead of the predicted 1000 guests a year, it drew 1500 visitors in the first week. According to legend, one of those first visitors ended up remaining at the lodge a lot longer than the weekend. In his book, *Ghosts, Critters and Sacred Places of Washington and Oregon II*, Jefferson Davis explains there is a ghost that haunts one room in particular and likes to taunt the employees in various parts of the lodge.

The ghost's name is Elisabeth and her story is a sad one. She came to the Oregon Caves Lodge as a newlywed on her honeymoon. Instead of the start of a joyful life with her new husband, Elisabeth got a terrible shock. As the story goes, she left her husband behind one day while she went exploring the network of trails near the lodge. She returned to find her husband in bed with a pretty chamber maid. Crushed by her love's infidelity, Elisabeth locked herself in the bathroom later that night and slit her wrists. Her ghost continues to haunt the room where she died, and other areas of the hotel.

Room 308 is where Elisabeth ended her life. There have been reports from some guests that her presence is palpable. They get an uneasy feeling in the room, as if someone is there. The sound of pacing up and down the hallway outside the room has been heard by guests staying in room 308, almost as if Elisabeth was waiting impatiently for them to leave. Some guests who went to investigate the sound found there was a sudden drop in the temperature outside the room.

The lodge employees are not exempt from Elisabeth's phantom activities. Some of the maids have had to refold their linens and towels several times because someone keeps turning their nicely folded piles of sheets into a big, crumpled mess. After they stack up the folded linens and leave to do other tasks, they return to find all their work on the floor in a heap.

The kitchen staff is aware that someone or something likes to keep them on their toes. The gas jets will be turned off for the night, but the cook has found them turned on full before going home at the end of the day. If it only happened once, they might blame themselves. However, the jets will be carefully turned off, only to be turned on again minutes later.

At the time of this writing, the lodge had been closed since the fall of 2001, so I couldn't check with current employees or guests about the ghostly goings-on.

The Ghosts of the Great Hall

A former employee at the Sunriver Resort wrote to me about a ghost there. According to Shirley Stockwell, the ghost is said to be a soldier who served when the resort was known as Camp Abbot. As it turns out, he apparently still haunts the scenic vacation spot, which is tucked away amid the stately pines of Central Oregon at the foot of the Cascade Mountains.

The mystery, according to the company that handles publicity for Sunriver, resides in the Great Hall Ballroom and Conference Center. The hall is a massive open-beamed structure composed of 511 logs (150,000 feet of timber) with an imposing stone fireplace that fills one end of the two-story building from floor to ceiling. A circular staircase winds to the second-floor halls, which surround the main floor below. It's in the "crow's nest" or upper balcony where the mystery unfolds.

Sixty years ago, when the beautiful meadow was home to Camp Abbot (named after Lt. Henry Abbot), the Army Corps of Engineers carried out military exercises during World War II. The camp's proximity to the nearby Deschutes River provided important training opportunities for building bridges over rivers, an essential skill during that war.

In October 1943, construction began on Camp Abbot's Officer's Club, which is now the Great Hall. By the following April it was completed. Legend has it that during a training exercise, one of the enlisted men was killed accidentally.

Several current and former Sunriver Resort employees have reason to believe that the soldier still keeps watch over the Great Hall. While up in the crow's nest, a few people have seen a nattily dressed soldier wearing military fatigues and a heavy coat that match photos of Camp Abbot in the resort's archives.

Spirits usually appear for one of three reasons. If someone died suddenly or with little warning, as in the case of a traumatic accident, the spirit may not realize the person is dead. Or someone could be confined to this world by a broken promise made to a loved one. The third reason may be that he or she has some unfinished business, usually pertaining to a loved one. A variation of this reason would be if the person was killed at an untimely moment.

According to accounts by Doug Thompson of Hunter Public Relations, quite a few employees have come across the soldier ghost. A good example is Sam Degarmo, a custodian at Sunriver who has been working there for more than 11 years. Originally from Nebraska, Sam has lived in Oregon since 1936.

Early one December morning, while cleaning up the conference center, Sam and a co-worker saw a candelabra fly off the top of a piano and crash to the floor. "We were the only ones in the room," says Sam. "There was no reason for it to go anywhere. Something moved it." He has other similar examples of what he calls "weird things happening in the Great Hall that aren't supposed to happen." Again, it was close to Christmas. "There seems to be more activity at that time of year." Sam was walking along a hallway lined with tables covered in holiday decorations. Suddenly one of the tree boughs started waving back and forth. There was no draft or breeze to cause the movement.

A couple of years ago, Sam's duties included cleaning the restrooms. He checked one of the ladies' room stalls and found it needed toilet paper. After getting some, he returned

The Great Hall at Sunriver Resort, long haunted by a soldier in military fatigues

to find the stall locked. "I had to crawl underneath the door to unlock it. I don't know how it happened since I was the only one there."

A security guard told Sam about several sightings of a man in military uniform in the window of the hall. The guard would inspect the building from top to bottom, but never found anyone. Another worker told Sam of an early morning shift that spooked him. Bob was trying to push open a swinging door to get into the hall from the kitchen, but it wouldn't budge. He shoved on it several times, thinking someone was playing a prank by blocking it from the other side. The door finally gave, but there was no one in sight when Bob went through.

Kathy Tilley hasn't had any unusual experiences in her 27 years to confirm the ghost's existence, but she has heard from more than a few co-workers who have encountered something. "We had one cook who wouldn't even go in there, he was so afraid of what he would see," says Kathy. The native of Bend says her father was stationed at Camp Abbot in the early 1940s. "I can feel a presence in there when I'm there alone in the mornings, but others have actually seen a soldier up in the balcony area."

Shirley Stockwell, an employee for some 22 years, never got to see him either. But she also says many of her former colleagues saw a man in a full-length coat and military boots roaming the upper level of the hall. Although the war ended long ago, it's possible that one soldier who never made it to the front persists in wandering. Unaware that the war is over, he still hopes to rejoin his comrades at arms.

3

Public Phantoms
and
Local Legends

Ghosts of East Medford

As much as ghosts can be frightening, they can also be a source of community pride. The people of Medford certainly delighted in the entity that roamed through their town. The following account was printed in the *Medford Sun* in 1911.

Ghosts! The residents of the east side near the bridge have been seeing one. The ghost is of the regulation kind, being white and having the faculty of doing unexplainable things.

As the clock in the belfry of the old water tower tolls the hour of three and the owl flutters back to his place to prepare for the coming of dawn, from the battlements of Bear Creek Bridge there emerges the ghost.

The ghost would apparently hesitate for a moment before it turned and hurried across the field adjacent to the Pacific and Eastern tracks, its feet scarcely touching the earth and its whole body a swirling white ball. The report says the ghost was "contemptuous of man-made fences, houses and freight cars" as it continued its headlong dash. It would disappear in the dusk, a fast-moving white speck that revolved over and over into the depths of darkness.

The residents of East Medford could count on a repeat performance by the specter every night of the week except Sunday. Residents who had heard the queer sound it made in its flight would be sure to watch for it in the hopes of seeing it as well. Despite a concerted communal effort, they never saw any more than that just described.

The article continues: "No chickens, watermelons, nor money have been missed, however, and the motive of the strange creature is still in doubt." People living near the bridge even considered turning their dogs loose, but after one attempt the idea was abandoned. The only animal ever sent out on a ghost hunt returned cowering at the first appearance of the specter.

That didn't seem to bother the citizens of East Medford. As the *Medford Sun* reported, "The east side is taking much local pride in the ghost, and if it continues its efforts to give night séances at three o'clock it may become firmly established."

Perhaps the people of Medford can let us know if they still see their ghost by the Bear Creek Bridge. A spirit so revered might just stick around.

The Hunchback of Chautauqua

The discovery of a Clovis-point arrowhead near Lithia Park in 1996 suggests its owners may have dated back to the Ice Age. But ghosts of a much more recent era have been seen, heard and smelled in the Ashland park.

The eight-acre park, founded in 1892 by the Chautauqua Association, brought entertainment and culture to southern Oregon. The Chautauqua Series was a national educational program begun in 1874 by Methodists Lewis Miller and John Heyl Vincent. It involved traveling lectures and music that kept people amused in the days before radio and television. Visitors came from miles around over the next thirty summers to participate in the various attractions offered, and to camp in what was to become Lithia Park.

One of the most widely discussed spirits in Lithia Park is a hunchbacked boy with a very hairy face and body. Locals call him the Dog-Faced Boy. The son of a woodcutter, he apparently lived in the 1920s. In addition to his physical abnormalities, the boy was mentally challenged. He made a living selling pencils and stealing from the parked wagons and cars of people attending the Oregon sessions of the Chautauqua Series. The boy disappeared in the mid-1920s. His body was never found and no charges were ever laid, though people suspected he became a target of one of his vengeful victims.

In the 1960s, an apparition with the hunched and hairy physique of the boy was seen carrying a bag over his shoulder and rummaging through the cars parked in the lot for the local Shakespeare festival, which replaced the Chautauqua Series. But whenever someone approached the furtive shape, it disappeared. There were more sightings in the 1980s and

An early photo of Lithia Park, where a hunchbacked ghost known as the Dog-Faced Boy terrorizes visitors

again in the mid 1990s. Local police were called out to investigate. Each time they find nothing.

Naturally, the story changes each time it is relayed, and the misshapen soul has been accused of leaping at people and scaring them. For the most part, however, he seems content to rifle through the contents of parked cars. It would be interesting to know if he can get in without setting off those sensitive car alarms.

Another ghost in the park is that of a young girl who was raped and murdered in 1875. A blue light thought to be the energy of her spirit is often seen floating through the park at night. Some who have passed through the light say they felt a cold chill.

A third ghost, of a logger who was killed by a falling tree, is reported to have saved lives. Jefferson Davis tells the story in his *Ghosts and Strange Critters of Washington and Oregon.* In the early 1900s, water rich in lithium—now known as Lithia water—bubbled from the town's fountains. The man drank a lot of the local water out of a jug that he carried. When it was empty, he would play the jug like an instrument. Two loggers were saved in separate incidents from falling logs. Just before they were pushed or pulled out of harm's way, both men say they heard the sound of a man playing a jug and they smelled a sulfurous odor—a result of drinking too much of the lithium-rich water.

Rock Point Cemetery

The term "ghost town" usually refers to formerly inhabited enclaves that, for whatever reason, have been abandoned. But in Jackson County, locals take the phrase literally. A dark hooded entity wanders through the Rock Point Pioneer Cemetery in one of southern Oregon's true ghost towns.

Back in 1860, Rock Point was a bustling community with schools, churches, stores, a post office and blacksmith's shop. When the town was bypassed as a train station, most people moved to nearby Gold Hill, leaving behind the tombs of their deceased relatives. Now all that remains is the cemetery and perhaps a specter or two.

There are stories of a hooded ghost that carries a lantern as it roams among the overgrown tombstones and vanishes into thin air when approached. Other tales exist of strange lights, sounds and visions of fire leaping from the crypts. A greenish fog has also been reported in the area, and the story goes that anyone driving through it risks having his or her car windows broken. Some locals believe the hauntings are a direct result of the Oregon Vortex, which is located in nearby Gold Hill. (The Vortex is a well-documented phenomenon that appears to distort space and distance.) It is also possible that the restless spirits of those left behind still wander the cemetery, unhappy that their loved ones departed without them.

The Legend of Crater Lake

In the Cascade Mountains, perched 6000 feet above the rest of Oregon, is a secret treasure. Crater Lake is a sapphire jewel, nestled in the hollow shell of a shattered volcano. Many explorers missed it because the lake is hidden from sight until you crest the volcano's rim. There are two explanations for how the lake was formed—the geological and the legendary.

About 7000 years ago, scientists say a 12,000-foot volcanic mountain stood where the lake is now. The mountain, posthumously named Mount Mazama, erupted violently—an eruption 42 times as powerful as the 1980 eruption of Mount St. Helens. It spewed volcanic ash and pumice lava over the region, emptying the cavernous magma chamber below the surface. With the mountain's underlying support weakened, the mountain collapsed and formed a basin or caldera. The lava continued to flow, sealing the bottom of the basin, which allowed it to fill with rainfall and snow melt to create the deepest lake in the United States and the seventh deepest lake in the world at 1932 feet.

The pristine waters remained unknown to white men until explorer John Wesley Hillman came upon the lake by accident in 1853. Hillman, Henry Klippel and Isaac Skeeters were in search of the legendary "Lost Cabin" gold mine. Hillman reported that it was the bluest lake he had ever seen. Local Klamath Indians had known of it long before recorded history but considered it a sacred place. They refused to acknowledge its existence to outsiders. In fact, up until Hillman stumbled upon the lake, Indian guides hired by other explorers had been carefully led around the five-mile wide crater. Hillman wrote that the Indians believed that gazing upon the waters was fatal. The shamans forbade anyone from climbing up the crater's edge to peer inside.

William Gladstone Steel is credited with founding Crater Lake National Park in 1902. Steel first learned of the enchanted place from a newspaper article that was wrapped around his lunch. After seeing the lake for himself, he devoted his life and fortune to preserving such a remarkable site.

Although explorers and scientists have studied the origins of the lake from an academic perspective, the Klamath Indian legends suggest it had a supernatural source. The best known legend describes the war between Llao, chief spirit of Crater Lake and god of the Below-world, and Skell, a mighty spirit of Klamath Marsh to the south and god of the sky.

The demon king Llao would often stand on top of Mount Mazama to survey the earth. One day, Llao spied the beautiful daughter of the Klamath chief and immediately wanted her for his wife. He came down from his throne and confronted the maiden, asking her to join him and rule by his side. She rejected him because he was ugly and came from the Below-world. Llao tried to get the Klamath chief to consent to a marriage, but he also refused, saying his daughter had been ordained by the gods as the next chief of his people and he could not allow her to leave.

Furious, Llao swore he would take revenge on the Klamath people. He climbed to the top of his mountain and launched a vicious assault, hurling fire down on the Indians. The Klamath chief beseeched Skell for help, and the sky god—who also adored the lovely daughter—descended to defend the helpless humans.

The ensuing battle between Llao and Skell shook the earth. The gods threw red rocks as large as hills, making the ground tremble and causing landslides of fire. A terrible darkness spread over the land for days. Llao's demon army took advantage of the dark to attack Skell and killed him. The demon warriors maliciously cut Skell's heart out of his body and carried it up to Llao Rock for a celebration. But Skell's followers, led by the Klamath chief's daughter, cleverly stole the heart back and restored it to Skell's body, bringing the god back to life.

During the last great battle, Skell defeated Llao and killed him. The sky god ordered the body be cut up and thrown into the lake to be devoured by the giant crawfish and other monsters that dwelled in the deep waters. The evil creatures were loyal to Llao, but they were easily fooled into eating his remains. Skell tricked them by shouting "Here are Skell's arms" as he tossed the limbs into the water. The horrible beasts gobbled up the various body parts, including the legs and torso. But when Skell flung Llao's head into the lake, the water creatures realized they had been tricked and wouldn't touch it. The head magically transformed into the rock now known as Wizard Island.

Many people still believe Llao's spirit continues to live within Llao Rock, a massive cliff of black obsidian along the rim of the lake. Sometimes, when a sudden storm interrupts a peaceful day, it is thought that Llao's restless spirit whips up an angry gale, turning the lake into a churning cauldron.

Another myth suggests that Llao's underwater creatures are still lurking in the lake's depths. One such creature, the giant crayfish, plucks unwary visitors from the crater rim and drags them to their deaths in the dark, chilly water. For adventurous hikers, it might be worth the extra effort to register with the park authority if you plan to stay at the lake overnight—just in case.

The Old Clatsop Hospital

Initially, the only reference I could find to hauntings at the old Clatsop Hospital in Astoria was an Internet listing of Oregon's haunted places. But when I called what is now the Clatsop Care Center, a nursing home and assisted-living center to confirm the story, the person who answered the phone promptly told me that the ghost's name is George.

The hospital was built in 1926, but by 1976 the newer Columbia Hospital had opened and the building became vacant. A group of concerned citizens organized a movement to preserve the old hospital. It was renovated and converted to a long-term care center in 1979, though some the original structure, such as the elevator that descends to the morgue, remained in use. Employees on the night shift have seen an apparition walking the halls.

There are several tales involving the laundry room. I spoke to Anita, the center's administrator since 1991, who says that several members of the staff were in a tizzy over laundry carts that would disappear. One story involved a blonde nurse in an old-fashioned uniform who was seen one night getting on the elevator with a laundry cart. Two hospital employees ran down the stairs to confront whoever was taking their cart. When they reached the ground floor by the morgue, the

George, a deceased former patient, is the resident spirit at this nursing home in Astoria.

elevator had arrived. They couldn't have been more shocked when they opened the old cage-style doors. Inside, the cart was making a solo ride. No woman was in the elevator. With a growing body of evidence suggesting that something was upsetting the staff, Anita decided to call a priest and have him spread holy water throughout the laundry area. It seemed to do the trick. Reports of ghostly activity stopped.

● ● ●

George was a patient on the residential care floor. When Anita worked as a social worker at the hospital in the 1980s, she used to sit with people while they were dying. But George was an atheist who didn't believe in an afterlife.

Anita didn't know what to do for him, so she put on some peaceful music. "I tried to comfort him as best I could. He died later that night."

Anita then had a few days off. The minute she came back to work, she heard from the other hospital staff that the night after George died the light went on in his room. The floor attendant turned it off, but it would turn back on. This happened four or five nights in a row. Anita told her colleague, "Maybe George is telling us there is life after death after all." After that, the incidents stopped.

A Jailhouse Ghost

This quirky story comes from an article published in the *Oregon Sentinel* on February 27, 1886. Under the heading "The Haunted Jail," the Jacksonville paper reported that the deputy sheriff believed the prison was occupied by ghosts. "Strange noises are heard and sights seen, which are bloodcurdling." I was unable to find out more about the bloodcurdling sights, but the speculation was that the ghost was a convicted murderer who had starved himself to death. The dead killer was named Bardon. He had been sentenced to hang for killing a sheep-herder from the Rogue River area and eating his whole flock. While in prison, Bardon refused any nourishment until he was nothing more than a skeleton. Some good-hearted women attempted to feed the dying prisoner, but he refused and subsequently died in his cell.

In a related article printed the same day, the paper reported that the ghost was not Bardon but the spirit of "that dead Chinaman," who had been having a lot of fun in one of the back cells of the county jail.

The article continued, "The ghost appears to be a very active and lively one and not afraid of work as he invariably either turns everything upside down or changes its position in one way or another."

The guards watching over a sentenced murderer being kept in the jail—a man named O'Neil—said they hadn't seen the ghost. To quell the speculation, a group of five "representative citizens" visited the jail to examine the cell where the ghostly activity had taken place. They found the cell empty. Thinking this an opportunity to prevent future hauntings, the group devised a plan to keep the ghost away. They fastened the cell door and small window shut with sealing wax and "mosquito bar." That seemed to have the desired effect— the ghost didn't show up once the door was sealed. Surprisingly, the editorial comment from the newspaper at the end of the article suggested the efforts were unlikely to succeed for long. "If we are any judge of his strength...we will just bet our last nickel that there won't be a bit of mosquito bar left and the seal on the wax will be ruined forever. We anxiously await developments."

It's been more than 116 years since that declaration.

The Oregon Vortex

Since it was discovered, physicists, paranormal experts and documentary producers have flocked to a cabin on Sardine Creek. Everyone agrees on one thing—there's something unusual here. People appear shorter or taller depending on where they stand. Photos are distorted. Trees and people incline toward magnetic north, as if pulled by some invisible force.

The Oregon Vortex is a circular piece of ground 165 feet in diameter. It is in the southern part of the state between Medford and Grant's Pass on Sardine Creek Road. Indian lore tells of this strange place long before the white man came. Native American horses, for instance, refused to go into the affected area, so the Indians shunned it and called it the "Forbidden Ground."

In 1904, the Old Gray Eagle Mining Company built an assay office there, and it later became a tool storage shed. Positioned almost in the center of the vortex, the structure became known as the "House of Mystery." The unusual conditions were well noted. But it wasn't until John Litster, a geologist and mining engineer, developed the area in 1929 that the disturbance became public knowledge. By 1930, it was a full-blown tourist attraction.

The Oregon Vortex website defines the phenomenon as a spherical field, half above and half below ground. A vortex is a natural whirlpool of force, like water going down a drain or a tornado. As such, it creates a very odd set of circumstances. Visual perspective, for example, is altered so that people appear taller when facing magnetic north and shorter when facing magnetic south.

Italian-born John Litster originally came from England to conduct mining surveys. The son of a British foreign

The Oregon Vortex. Despite appearances, the platform in both photographs above is level. The House of Mystery is pictured in the background.

diplomat, Litster was a well-educated engineer. The anomalies around the old cabin captured his attention and he soon became absorbed in revealing the truth behind the vortex. He felt the strange energy was actually warping space and time. His experiments are on display at the vortex and on the vortex website. Pictures show two people standing on a level concrete slab. The person standing in the vortex is always shorter than the one outside the vortex. When the people switch positions, the one who was previously shorter becomes taller and vice versa.

Litster conducted thousands of experiments until his death in 1959. Much of his work, however, was lost. There is a small publication called *Notes and Data* containing some of his work. It is on sale at the visitor center.

Ultimately, there are only theories about the cause of the phenomena; no real explanations exist. In some of his experiments, Litster created a series of illusions using principles of light and angles. His theory was that the vortex acted as a huge lens. As light travels through the area, it bends, refracts or distorts, causing it to travel in a vertical or circular motion rather than a straight line. Some of the effects, in particular the blurring effect on photographs, remain a mystery. Needless to say, the vortex continues to be a big attraction for thrill-seekers.

Ruth, the Ghost of Umatilla County Library

The death of Miss Ruth Skiff Cochran made the front page of the *Pendleton East Oregonian* in October 1947. Umatilla's assistant county librarian died quite suddenly at age 53, and her death shocked a community that had come to like and respect her through her 23 years of dedicated service. One of the highest tributes paid to Ruth came from Neva LeBlond, head of the Umatilla County Library, who says: "To most people in Umatilla County, Miss Cochran is the library." And it appears Ruth remained attached to her stacks of books well after her untimely death.

Rumors persist as to how Ruth came to haunt her beloved library. Stories circulated that she poisoned herself with lye because of a failed love affair. According to her obituary, however, the reference librarian was conscious when she was found Sunday afternoon in the library basement. She apparently told ambulance attendants that she had felt ill Saturday when she closed the library, so she went to the basement to rest before her long walk home, but became so ill she was unable to summon help. The newspaper states that Ruth was rushed to St. Anthony's hospital and died of a cerebral hemorrhage. Strange things started happening after Miss Cochran's demise.

One janitor was convinced that books jumped off the shelves at him when no one else was there. Librarians working at night have heard the footsteps of an unseen visitor pacing through the aisles of books. Windows have opened by themselves and lights have turned on and off. Mary Finney, Pendleton's current librarian, says she doesn't necessarily believe the reports of Ruth's postmortem activity, but admits there are some interesting sounds in the old building.

In 1996, the library moved to an old junior high school about five blocks from the original location. Mary Finney says it doesn't appear that Ruth followed. There have not been any incidents in the new Pendleton library.

After several years of renovation work, a new arts center opened in April 2001 in the old library building on Main Street. The executive director of the Pendleton Center for the Arts is Delta Smith. She says she's a skeptic but is open to the idea of Ruth. Delta claims there have not been any strange noises or evidence of a ghostly presence for a few years now. She has not seen anything ghostly, not even during many late nights of working alone in the building. She also points out that with the renovation and relocation, all of the things that Ruth's spirit may have been connected to are gone, including the washroom where she was found dying. Perhaps once the books were removed, Ruth realized it was time to leave too.

Sears Hall,
U.S. Army Reserve Center

This might be the least likely place to look for ghost stories. The U.S. Army, after all, doesn't often encourage such superstition. But the Sears Army Reserve Drill Hall in Portland is said to be haunted by the spirit of the soldier for whom it is named.

The hall is dedicated to the memory of Jerome F. Sears, Sergeant First Class. An Oregon native, Sears was born in 1928 and enlisted in 1950. He was sent to fight in Korea in 1951. A year later, he was ordered to lead his men to a hill near Sidamak, Korea, and hold the area. On June 9, 1952, the regiment was hit by an intense enemy attack. Sears was badly wounded, but he stayed behind to help his men. When the enemy soldiers advanced, Sears ordered his detachment to retreat. He stayed behind with another soldier to provide cover fire as the others retreated. When the company regrouped and counter-attacked, it was too late. Sears and the other soldier were already dead.

Sears was awarded the Distinguished Service Cross, the second highest distinction given by the U.S. Army. A military facility in Korea was named Camp Sears in his honor and Portland's Army Reserve Center became Sears Hall. It's not known if Sergeant Sears visits the Korean camp named after him, but some of the soldiers in Oregon believe his ghost may be responsible for some of the odd things that happen at Sears Hall.

Jeff Davis, one of Oregon's most prolific ghost story writers, also did a stint in the military and knew some of the soldiers at Sears Hall. In his book, *Ghosts, Critters and Sacred*

Places of Washington and Oregon, Davis recounts their experiences. One soldier, Supply Sergeant Jones, had reason on more than one occasion to run out into the drill hall to catch the person rattling the lockers. The drill hall was lined with metal wall lockers, and the culprit would hit them as he walked along, making the locks rattle. In a big concrete hall, the din would echo quite loudly. But every time Sergeant Jones ran out to tell the person to stop, she would find herself alone and the noise would cease. It could have been a prank, except for the time when she actually saw the metal garage door rattling, as if someone on the other side wanted to get in. She hurried to open the door next to the big garage door. As soon as she looked outside, the banging stopped. But there was no one there.

On the second floor, people working at night have heard the sound of someone walking down the hall in rubber-soled boots. When they investigated, they found the floor empty. One particularly vigilant major thought someone was playing a prank, so he waited in the stairwell for the mischief-maker to come downstairs. No one did. So he went back up and walked around the second floor. There wasn't another soul there. Was it the spirit of Sergeant Sears? The major could still feel a presence and he noticed that lights in the building flickered. He went out into the vacant hallway and looked out a west window at the sunset. When he turned back, he saw the silhouette of a man in the window of a door to an office across the hall from his own office. Thinking it might be his shadow from rays of the setting sun, the major bobbed and weaved. He spotted his own shadow but the figure of the other man, who appeared to sport a military hair cut, did not move. The major went to where the person might have been and saw nothing. But when he reached out to touch a chair in the area, the hair on his arm stood on end. He felt a little charge like static electricity. After the major asked Sears to take care of the building, he quickly left.

Although Sergeant Sears died thousands of miles from home, it may be that he recognizes the honor bestowed on him by his comrades and feels comfortable in a place that bears his name.

Yaquina Bay Lighthouse— Haunted or Hoax?

Mysterious lights in the old tower. Sightings of a red-haired sailor with a gleaming skull for a face. Bloodcurdling screams during tempests. Ghost stories swirl about the Yaquina Bay Lighthouse, which shut down in 1874. In tracing the stories of odd occurrences on Oregon's central coast, I discovered a lot of fiction mixed up with what is often taken for historical fact. Even so, there are enough accounts of disturbing events to cause a shiver while alone in the old building.

The lighthouse was only three years old when the U.S. Lighthouse Service closed it and locked the doors. The large Cape Cod-style structure, with its 40-foot tower and whale oil lantern, was built in a poor location. Its warning beams were barely visible from sea. The Yaquina Head Lighthouse three and a half miles up the coast replaced it. Since then, the lighthouse, which is one of the few Pacific Coast lighthouses that also houses the lightkeeper's quarters, has been used at various times by the U.S. Army Engineers and Coast Guardsmen, the predecessor to the U.S. Coast Guard.

In 1946, bulldozers were set to mow the building down, but Lincoln County residents formed a human chain around

After it closed it 1874, Yaquina Bay Lighthouse became a hotbed of paranormal sightings—some more credible than others.

the crumbling foundation in protest. Their efforts saved the lighthouse, which was eventually restored by the state and turned into a museum.

The eerie stories started almost immediately after the lighthouse closed. Apparently, a phantom sailor moved in as soon as the coast was clear. In Newport, some say it is the ghost of Evan MacClure, the violent captain of the American whaler *Moncton,* whose crew staged a mutiny and set him adrift in a small boat. He was never seen alive again, but a boat much like his washed up just down the coast on the rugged rocks of Devil's Punchbowl. There have been sightings of a man in sailor's clothing with bright red hair prowling the beach in front of the lighthouse, as well as calls for help at sea with no source. Rattlings were heard in cellars and footsteps tromped through attics. According to local legend, the minute the two-story house with the light above it became vacant, MacClure's ghost moved in and the rattlings and creepy noises on the beach stopped.

Then there is the story of young Muriel Trevenard, who was supposedly killed in the lighthouse in December 1874. Visitors still ask to see the bloodstains that were reported to mark the floor where she met her horrible death. Unexplained lights have been seen at night in the empty tower. The stories of Muriel's ghost and her haunting came from a fictional short story in an 1899 issue of *Pacific Monthly*.

The author, Lischen M. Miller, captured people's imaginations with her flowery prose. Miller was married to George Melvin Miller, the brother of poet Joaquin Miller who wrote a series of poems published in 1871 entitled *Songs of the Sierras*. George and Lischen lived in Eugene, where he was a real estate promoter. During her short life—she died quite young—Lischen Miller wrote a compelling tale of a luckless sea captain who left his sweet-natured daughter in a Newport rooming house while he sailed the ocean.

In Miller's story, the delicate and bored main character, Muriel, takes up with a group of fun-loving tourists who decide to explore the deserted lighthouse. Inside they find a mysterious shaft that drops into a seemingly bottomless well hidden behind a panel in a small room between the second story and the lantern tower.

When the group leaves the lighthouse, Muriel realizes she has lost her handkerchief. She goes back alone to retrieve it.

Her new friends wait until "the somber stillness of the darkening day was rent by a shriek so wild and weird that they who heard it felt the blood freeze suddenly in their veins." The terrified group rushes back, only to find "a pool of warm, red blood. There were blood drops in the hall and on the stairs that led up to the landing..." Muriel had vanished. Her bloodstained handkerchief lays on the floor.

Miss Miller told her story so well that everyone since, from local teachers to tour guides, have retold and embellished it. At a Rotary Club meeting, one Newport local who knew fact from fiction listened to someone suggest that if a person could be at the lighthouse at the right time, it would be possible to hear Muriel's ghost moaning. In fact, one professor at Oregon State University used to tell his students the story without mentioning it was fictional.

So how does one explain the strange goings-on reported at the lighthouse? In a 1975 article in the *Register-Guard*, Pat Stone, then curator of the Lincoln County Historical Museum, told a reporter of several unexplained incidents that she had experienced. When she was alone in the house on a gray foggy night, Pat Stone heard footsteps upstairs. The sound stopped when someone came to tour the building.

The Coast Guard staff has seen lights in the tower when it was supposed to be locked and empty. Pat Stone says a lone figure carrying a lantern has been spotted out on the beach in front of the lighthouse, but when the guardsmen turned a floodlight on, no one was there.

The story that convinced Mrs. Stone of ghosts in the area came from a young hitchhiker who was out of work and desperate for a job. He had nowhere to go, so he slept in his sleeping bag in front of the lighthouse. He saw the apparition of a young girl floating above the ground outside one of the upper windows. The beautiful ghost told him not to worry because he would find work the following day. Pat Stone says the young man did find work the next day. And she believes he had no reason to make up the story, because he didn't know the place was rumored to be haunted.

Today, the refurbished lighthouse offers regular tours. It's even possible to have a wedding there. In 1996, additional restoration work allowed the relighting of the tower—this time with a photocell to provide steady white light from dusk until dawn. Current staff members haven't experienced anything unusual lately, but they happily tell guests about the area and building history. Most of the footsteps nowadays are from groups of school children pounding through the rooms.

The Uppertown
Firehouse Ghost

The Uppertown Firefighters Museum in Astoria used to be the fire station. Back when it was a functioning station, the fire engines were parked on the ground level, volunteer firefighters' rooms were on the second floor and a youth club occupied the third floor. It's well known locally that one of the firefighters still lives there on the third floor, perhaps waiting for the next call.

The historic 1896 building was designed by the famous Portland architect Emil Schacht. Originally, it was part of the popular North Pacific Brewery until it closed during Prohibition. In 1928, the city of Astoria rebuilt the structure as the Uppertown Fire Station #2; it was retired in 1960. The city then donated the building and much of the classic equipment to the Clatsop County Historical Society in 1989.

Martha works for the Clatsop Historical Society. She knows all the stories and she has heard the ghost herself. The museum is usually closed through the winter and spring, but she recalls waiting for a pre-arranged group tour in spring 2001. She was standing next to desk when she clearly heard someone walk across the floor upstairs. "I really didn't believe it at first. I heard the footsteps, so I called up. There was no answer." Martha didn't investigate but she knew there was no one else in the building.

Martha also knew a volunteer who worked at the museum every weekend for many years. The man spent many hours there alone and said he often heard the footsteps above. As the story goes, it is the ghost of a firefighter who fell down a brass pole and died, even though the tragedy happened at a different fire station. Firefighter Paul Marion died in 1928 after he fell through the hole while sleepwalking at the old fire station on Astor and Fourth Street. The station was torn down years ago. Perhaps the dead firefighter moved into the Uppertown station because it was a familiar environment. Or maybe it is the spirit of someone else. Either way, the ghost is harmless. "He never does anything but walk around," says Martha. "He doesn't rearrange things or come downstairs."

Former acting chief Dick Williams spent many nights in the dormitory on the second floor, but he never saw a ghost. In an article published by the museum, however, he admits that there were some strange noises up there at night and funny things did happen. "Sometimes it was so noisy you couldn't believe it," Williams recalls. "Whoever was up there was dragging stuff across the floor. Something was floating around upstairs in that gymnasium for sure."

One morning, he remembers being awakened by his colleague Sid Larson at about 4 AM. Sid told him that he had been jolted out of sleep by someone standing by his bed staring at him. The pair searched the entire building and, as usual, found nothing.

After the Uppertown Fire Station was retired in 1960, the building was used for equipment storage. That meant the oil furnace had to continue running to keep the space dry. It was a cranky old unit and someone had to go in every day to check on it for the night. Dick Williams says people would come back spooked by weird noises upstairs.

The stories prompted the firefighters to start a pool of $10 each to pay someone to go up there and sleep overnight. No one ever did.

4

Haunted
Houses

Herman Helms House

Herman Helms House is marked by tragedy. Perhaps that is why the two ghosts that haunt it are always heard crying. There is the ghost of a woman who some say is Augusta Helms, Herman's wife, who walks the upstairs hallways weeping. And there is the ghost of her daughter Herminne, known locally as Minnie, who cries inconsolably at the bottom of the stairs.

Patriarch Herman Helms moved to Jacksonville in 1856. The German native was a baker and saloon keeper by trade. The Table Rock Billiard Saloon, which he opened with partner John Wintjen, was one of Jacksonville's most successful and longest running businesses. In April 1862, Herman married Augusta Engelbrecht. Within five years, they had three children, the youngest of whom died of smallpox. At the time of her death in December 1868, Minnie was only 22 months old. She was buried in a small grave in front of the family's log house.

By 1878, the family had swelled to include five more children. Herman built a beautiful two-story addition on the front lawn that was described as "one of the most elegant residences in town." Local legend says it sits atop his daughter's grave. That could explain why Minnie's ghost comes back now and then to haunt the house that still stands on South Oregon Street.

Some previous owners don't believe there's a ghost. Hugh and Cathy Brown heard all about the spooky stories when they bought the property, but they told a reporter for the *Oregonian* that they didn't have any problems with unwanted phantom houseguests.

Bill Cotrell, however, swears the house is haunted. His

Herman Helms House in Jacksonville, where weeping ghosts reflect the weight of family tragedy

experience left him with the unshakable belief that the spirit of one of the Helmses continues to grieve—and quite loudly. Cotrell didn't own the house, but he stayed there for three nights to watch the place and feed the dog for his friend Al Humpert, who was away on business. Cotrell says he was up late reading one night when he heard the sound of a woman crying near the front parlor. It was a wail that even made the dog whimper. Had someone, perhaps a homeless person, wandered in off the street? Cotrell checked the entryway, found it empty and went back to bed. Minutes later, the crying began again. "This time it was deep sobbing," Cotrell recalls. It scared the dog so much, it hid under the bed. When Cotrell told his friend about the strange sounds, he said he had heard it too and believed it to be Minnie's mother Augusta, who still mourns her young daughter's death.

At least one Jacksonville historian says there's no truth to the grave myth. Ray Lewis says early records indicate that Herman Helms bought a plot in the Jacksonville cemetery and moved his daughter's grave before building the larger house. When the new headstone was erected, the old grave marker was stored in the basement. Maybe that old marker is enough to remind Minnie's spirit where her home had been.

Although the facts suggest Minnie's grave is not under the house, others have seen the image of an old lady crying in one of the front rooms. Some people think it's Minnie, who has returned as an adult in search of her family.

Author Mike Helm chronicles the rest of the family's wretched history in his book *Oregon's Ghosts and Monsters*. Tragedy struck the Helms family again in 1888. This time, typhoid claimed the lives of the two teenage daughters, Matilda and Bertha. Then, in 1907, more disaster. The estranged husband of daughter Emma shot and killed her, wounded her sister Anna and then killed himself. Herman fortunately didn't witness the last calamity—he died in June 1899 and was remembered as a "loving husband, kind father, good neighbor and worthy citizen."

With so many deaths in the family, perhaps Jacksonville's crying ghosts are simply expressing perpetual sadness at such terrible losses.

Applegate House

Shannon Applegate grits her teeth when people talk about ghosts in her house. The great-granddaughter of Charles Applegate now lives next door to the family's pioneer homestead. She is both intimately connected to her past and very protective of it.

Charles Applegate built his farm in Yoncalla in 1852. He had moved to western Oregon from Missouri with his brothers, Jesse and Lindsay, in 1843. He had two wagons, each drawn by four oxen, and he also brought with him ten cows and one horse. Charles and his wife Melinda had 15 children who they raised in the home. The house is now a heritage building and is used for arts and education workshops. Shannon Applegate lived in the house during the 1970s. She eventually wrote a book, *Skookum: An Oregon Pioneer Family's History and Lore*, which chronicles her family's history. But her interpretation differs from that of the average local ghost legend.

"People do feel the presence of the past there," she says. "It's benign energy, part of a very loving place." Shannon says Applegate House resonates with the history and energy of people from the past. "If somebody walks in and out of the same door and slams the screen 900 times in a lifetime or sits in a certain place on the porch, something may linger there—some energy. Sometimes I think it's like a change in the wind current when you feel these things. Suddenly, because the wind is coming from another direction, you can hear sounds from away far off," she continues. "Maybe they are always happening at once and what you hear then is echoes."

She goes on to say she doesn't think of them as ghosts or spirits. "I just think that I am experiencing residues of very old energy. Some of it comes from specific people."

Early pioneer Charles Applegate, whose former home is permeated with the energy of family history

Those people are Shannon's ancestors. When she moved into the house, she could hear them arguing upstairs. The distinct sound of a man's and a woman's voice in heated discussion could be heard even though she knew there was no one there. While writing her book about the Applegate family, Shannon felt an acute need to let her spirit family know that she intended to portray their history accurately. After she conveyed that, by talking to the empty space, the voices diminished.

Shannon and her family have witnessed other examples of the energy in the Applegate House. Empty chairs rock as though someone were sitting in them; the sound of babies crying and the smell of pipe smoke are sensed when neither is present. A vision of a woman dressed in white or a man in baggy pants drifts like a dandelion seed past someone's line of sight. To Shannon's way of thinking, these are not ghosts, but traces of sound and light that remain in the house. She dislikes the term "ghost" because it implies that a spirit has returned to create disruptions or cause trouble. Her sense is that the house is alive with the vibrations of former occupants, as if their life forces were trapped inside the building.

Shannon spoke with a reporter once in the 1970s about the presences at Applegate House. The resulting article infuriated Shannon, because she felt it trivialized her experience. She was horrified by the response. That article has since been reprinted in other publications, but she asked me not to use it. "It's not an aspect of the house history that I care to contribute to. I don't want people driving up to the house craning their necks." She says supernatural events still take place, but the difference is she now recognizes that telling stories about specific events can threaten the things she cares about, such as privacy and the security of her house.

"If there are spirits walking among us, there's probably a reason," she says.

John Palmer House

Once a dilapidated Victorian relic, John Palmer House has become an inner-city Portland landmark listed on the National Register of Historic Places. The beautifully gabled Queen Anne home looked better suited for a wrecking ball than a garden party when it was purchased in 1968 by Mary Sauter and her family. They rolled up their sleeves and got to work. A lot of elbow grease went into restoring the home to its original grandeur.

Renovation and remodeling are known to activate spirits that may have been resting quietly. Sometimes they don't like the changes, other times they are pleased to see their home being cared for and upgraded. After the work is completed, many spirits fade away. But some ghosts prefer to remain, perhaps to enjoy the spruced-up surroundings or to harass the occupants for disturbing their post-mortem snooze. At John Palmer House, the former is the case.

It started with the noises upstairs. The Sauters would hear someone walking around when they knew everyone was downstairs. Then the alarm system would be set off, although the upper floor was empty. A visiting psychic told the Sauters that the restless ghost was none other than a red-haired woman named Lottie, a former opera singer who lost her voice at the end of her career. Lottie lived in the house in the early 1900s and stayed connected to it because she left behind some of her theatrical trunks.

The noises continued, followed by actual sightings of a ghost. Members of the Sauter family and guests at the B&B saw a female apparition that was thought to be Lottie. A ghostly figure was also seen walking through the kitchen door. Someone else witnessed a ghost standing at the foot of the basement stairs.

After years as a bed and breakfast, the Sauters changed their operation to short-term rentals. I spoke to one former tenant who lived in John Palmer House until December 2001. He was surprised to hear about the ghost stories and says he didn't see a thing. Lottie, it seems, is not about to reveal herself to everyone who passes through the front door.

The house has recently been listed for sale. Initially, the Sauters had it listed with an agency, but they are now selling it privately. The next owners stand to inherit not only a historic building, but a home with a phantom singer. Maybe if she is coaxed with enough applause, the former diva might test out her well-rested vocal chords with an aria or two.

The Old Storm House

Barbara Haas remembers living through the Depression more vividly than most people. She and her family contended not only with the difficult economic times, but also with a terrifying haunted house.

Barbara and her family moved into the old Strum place, known as Storm House, in 1937. The white clapboard house was built by an old German and sat on a hill five miles south of Cornelius. It had a huge barn and was surrounded by massive cedar, fir and pine trees. The Haas family thought that a move out of the city would allow them to live off the land, even if it meant scavenging for nuts and berries. The need for a place was all the more pressing because they had a baby girl to raise.

In an article about the experience, Barbara wrote: "We moved into the old Storm place after getting permission from Alex Eischen, who owned another farm about a mile and a half away and farmed this place. We asked about the amount of rent he wanted, but to our amazement he could hardly keep a grin off his face or the twinkle from his eyes, like he had some secret, and he said he didn't want any rent." She and her husband were told they could live there as long as they could stand it. Without saying why, the old farmer didn't expect them to last very long in the house. Neighbors also laughed when they heard the Haas family intended to move into the old Storm house. "We were met with many open stares, embarrassed grins and shakes of the head. Evidently the house was well known."

The Haases moved in, accompanied by a cousin who would stay with them by turns to help cut wood. They made a living chopping up wood for burning, selling it at $2.50 a cord. It wasn't much, but it kept them fed and healthy. They even had a well by the side of the house that provided them with fresh water. They pumped it by hand and hauled it in for drinking, bathing, cooking and housecleaning. "The well was a deep one and echoed many sounds, like footsteps walking that never appeared." At first, they dismissed the sounds as nothing.

They still hadn't discovered why people were so shocked that they were living there. Eventually, the stories filtered through. A cousin of Barbara's husband and her family had lived there before the Haases, but they refused to talk about their experiences. The German man up the road told stories that explained a little more. He said rumor had it that the Strums were bootleggers and that a man had been killed on the stairway leading upstairs. There were also supposed to be trapdoors in some of the rooms. Sure enough, Barbara found three trapdoors that led to dug-out spaces below the floors. And the bloodstains were still visible on the steps. But they didn't believe in ghosts, so they didn't worry—at least not at first.

Then the noises started. "The first seemed to be these resounding footsteps that could be heard on the north side of the house where the pump sat. I would run out to meet whomever was there, glad for any company as the farms were a long way apart in those days, but no one would be there." The next incident involved the sound of someone chopping wood in the woodshed in the afternoon. Barbara recalls: "It would be the sound of measured chopping and I would dash out, thinking my husband had come home early. When I'd get to the woodshed, the chopping would stop. It would start up again when I got back to the house. So I'd think he'd just stepped outside for a minute and go running out again when the chopping started up again. This would go on and on until I wore my legs out." This went on as long as they lived there and there never was an explanation for it.

Inside the house, there were other ghosts moving about. Barbara heard the sound of men's footsteps that would travel from the bloodstained steps into the living room. There would be a pause, then the steps would return. The unseen walker would end his pacing at the trapdoor in the front room.

"That trapdoor was very 'active,' " says Barbara. "I often wondered if someone was buried there." The family noted that every afternoon at about three o'clock, there was an automatic reaction for anyone in the room to suddenly jerk their head toward the trapdoor. They became used to the odd reaction and would notice that guests responded in the same way. Even if the visitors didn't know where the hidden door was, their heads would turn to look at it at the appointed time. It made no sense, but Barbara came to accept it as part of living in the house.

The full moon brought out new ghosts. When the bright moon would cast a glow over the fields, Barbara and her family would hear footsteps of a young girl who seemed to be barefoot, walking from the back door through the kitchen, living room and into the south bedroom where the footsteps stopped by the window. Barbara could hear the sound of bare feet sticking to the floor and moving across it. What was more shocking is they actually saw the woman. An apparition, barefoot and adorned in a long, black cape, made two appearances. One night, while they were expecting a cousin who was arriving late, Barbara awoke to see a woman in a cape standing in the bedroom doorway. Thinking it was Ruby, she invited her to come in and sleep on the cot at the end of the room. The person didn't move or speak, so Barbara whispered again two or three times for her to come in. In the moonlight, she could clearly make out the shape of the woman in a long cape. No response. Barbara was feeling nervous, so she woke her husband. He also saw the woman. Barbara told him she wouldn't talk to her, so her husband swung a fist and the figure disappeared. They found out the next day that the cousin never arrived because she stayed late playing cards at a friend's house.

There were other peculiar things that came with living in the old Storm house. Barbara knew that the rats in the attic were responsible for some of the scrabbling noises that could be heard at night. But many footsteps were heard walking to the trapdoors. Some nights, a bizarre wind would extinguish the kerosene lamp although the air outside the house was still. They would relight the lamp, and the ghostly gust would put it out again. Barbara would play this game for an hour until finally the light would stay on. Perhaps it was a faulty wick, or maybe there were spirits that preferred to move about in the shadows.

As her daughter played with her toys, Barbara noticed that she would suddenly stop and stare as if something was there. They dubbed the ghost "Oscar" and he became one of her daughter's imaginary playmates.

There were a few more disturbing incidents before the Haases finally moved out of the house. On one occasion, the owner was supposed to be picking up some of the old prune dryers in the shed. It was one of the evenings when the wind kept blowing out the kerosene lamps. They returned from milking and heard pounding noises in the shed. Barbara's brother, who was there helping out, volunteered to help Mr. Eischen. He arrived only to find the shed empty. But for the rest of the night they could hear trays being lifted, more pounding and footsteps. It went on for about an hour. The next day, the owner said he never made it there because he'd found what he needed elsewhere. The Haases decided to keep silent about that one.

On other occasions, party guests would suddenly announce they were leaving without any explanation other than they didn't feel comfortable. Similarly, Barbara started to fear the barn. She would go in on a calm, sunny day and "the gates and partitions would slam shut with such force they would almost hit me. Such a force would scare the living daylights out of me." There were no springs on the hinges to make them snap shut, so Barbara could not find a reasonable explanation.

In 1939, the Haas family moved away. Barbara's husband found work and she was happy to leave the house. Soon after, the house burned down in a great blaze. Barbara believes the community gathered together and torched it to eliminate the dark energy that presided there. There's nothing there now, so there is no way of knowing if the spirit of Oscar and his ghostly brethren still walk restlessly among the pines and cedars.

The Creaking Mantel

A ranch house along the Rogue River has a rather unusual living room mantel. The central beam was taken from an old barn, but it came with a gruesome history that replays every year. As the story goes, the family who built the house discovered it during their housewarming party.

The guests were gathered around the fire at midnight. As the clock chimed, everyone suddenly heard loud creaking noises coming from within the room. The sounds seemed to be coming from the fireplace. There were also sounds of horses whinnying and stomping.

Such odd phenomena prompted some research into the origin of the mantel. It turned out that it was part of a beam used for an execution by hanging on the same date as the housewarming party. A gang of outlaws hanged a man at midnight, then fled by horse. On the anniversary of his death, the hanged man could be heard swinging from the rafters.

This oral account is included in Margaret Read MacDonald's *Ghost Stories of the Pacific Northwest.*

The Painter House

Ingrid Painter and her family have had more than a few odd experiences since moving to their farm. In 1996, they relocated to Linn County from Washington to restore and maintain a deteriorating 1848 farmstead.

The incidents began before Ingrid and her husband Alan moved in. They spent 18 months moving their possessions and animals to their new home. Ingrid tells me that during that time some of their things were moved prematurely, including a box of tax forms that they needed. "Since our daughter Lucy lived only 30 miles away, we asked to her go over to the house and retrieve the necessary paperwork from an upstairs closet."

While Lucy was upstairs rummaging through the tax box, her dog started to growl and bark. She thought perhaps the neighbors had come to investigate who was in the house. As this was going on, Lucy was on the phone to her parents because she couldn't find the papers that they wanted. Then Lucy heard the front door open. She said to her mother, "Hang on, there's someone at the front door." But when she went downstairs, there was no one around. Her dog continued to bark. Lucy told her parents something strange was going on and she wanted to leave before dark.

Several months later, again before the family moved in, another of Ingrid's daughters, Clare, went to the farm with her boyfriend. It was a cold, wet February. Ingrid had not mentioned Lucy's experience to Clare. So it was a bit of a surprise when Clare told her mother that she was sure someone had been moving around upstairs the night she and her boyfriend slept there. They had lit a fire and spent the night on the living room floor before going on a trip to the coast in

A watercolor of the historic Painter House, the site of many unexplained phenomena

the morning. But Clare said she heard movement upstairs throughout the night. Although Clare found the experience exciting, it terrified her boyfriend, who couldn't wait to get out of the house.

Ingrid and another daughter, Sally, met a stranger who came by while they were at the house unloading more of their things. A man drove up the lane and got out of his car to tell them his story. He and his girlfriend had been looking for a place to rent. They came to Ingrid's house and sat on the porch waiting for the real estate person to arrive and show them the house. When the agent never arrived, they realized they had the wrong address. But the man said while they were waiting they felt a powerful presence and asked Ingrid if she had noticed it. Convinced there was something unusual about the house, he made a special trip to tell the new owners.

After the Painters moved in, Clare experienced another strange event. She was spending time at her parents' place

while between jobs. One night while Claire was in bed reading, her dog suddenly pricked up its ears and the hair on its
back stood on end. The dog didn't move but began to make a
low growling noise. Although the bedroom door didn't have
a doorknob or latch at that point, it was closed shut. All of a
sudden, it swung open. Clare didn't see or feel anything, but
given past events, she decided to be friendly and welcomed
any unseen spirits to come in.

The most intriguing—and eerie—experience came during the first summer the family were in the house. Ingrid and
her husband were working pretty hard to get things fixed up.
It was a scorching day, with temperatures over 90 degrees.
Ingrid says, "I was exhausted so I told my husband I was
going to lie down, even if it was the middle of the day. He
said he'd stay outside and carry on."

Up in her bedroom, Ingrid lay down facing the front window, with her back to the door. "Pretty soon I felt my husband come and join me and we lay like spoons in a drawer.
My only thought was, *Oh, isn't that nice.*" When she awoke,
Ingrid was surprised that her husband had left without waking her, because she is usually a light sleeper. She concluded
that exhaustion caused her to sleep soundly. When Ingrid
found her husband working out back, she commented on
how quietly he left from their nap without even waking her.
"I don't know who you were sleeping with," he said. "But it
certainly wasn't me. I've been here all afternoon."

The experiences aren't limited to immediate family,
either. Ingrid's cousin and her husband came to stay once.
They slept in the middle bedroom upstairs. The cousin told
Ingrid that she took a blouse out of her suitcase and lay it on
the top so it wouldn't be wrinkled in the morning. The next
day, when they awoke, the blouse had been moved and lay

neatly over a box. Even the cousin's skeptical husband had trouble explaining that one.

Ingrid's fourth daughter, Katie, has told her several times that she has heard someone at night when she is sleeping in the same room where Clare had her door-opening incident. And on many occasions, the family dog just sits up suddenly and stares into one part of the house, growling softly. But Ingrid says she has never felt threatened or unwelcome in her home.

She researched the house's history and discovered that the original settlers were a man, Jonathan Keeney, and his wife, Mary. They lived in a cabin on the property from 1848 until the house was finished in 1852. Descendants of Jonathan tried to get the house on the historical register but failed because the original structure had been altered too much. It does have, oddly enough, the dubious acclaim of being one of the first places to be listed on the property tax list.

Although the strange happenings continue to make things interesting, Ingrid and Alan are quite happy not to dig any deeper. Ingrid says she really doesn't want to befriend whatever ghost might be living with them. She's content to share the space in peaceful harmony.

Buttertoes

The ghost's name is Lydia. Little is known about her, except that she was one of the original tenants in the Belmont-area house in Portland. She would sit in the window of her second-floor suite, rocking back and forth in her chair. Lydia lived there for 25 years until her death in the 1920s.

The Victorian home was built in 1893. After Lydia's death, it passed through several hands. In the late 1970s, it was remodeled and turned into the Buttertoes Restaurant. The restaurant was on the main floor, below the room in which Lydia lived. But Lydia's ghost refused to be confined to her old quarters. Her spectral image was said to appear, wearing a high-necked dress, whenever a disbeliever was in the room. Chairs would be rearranged and the odd muffin tin was said to fly through the air of its own accord. Some of the workers said they felt a presence standing behind them, so strong that it made them turn around to look, but they would be alone. There are stories that the restaurant owner came in to work one day to find the mail had been picked up off the floor, sorted and laid out on the counter.

Although the building is listed on most ghost hunter websites, there is a general belief in the paranormal research community that the haunting may be a hoax. The owner of Buttertoes moved to a new location in the early 1990s. The former Buttertoes Restaurant is now the very funky, almost bohemian Pied Cow Coffee House. Since the changeover, ghostly sightings in the old home have dropped to nil.

"We've all been really happy here," says Melinda, one of the coffee house employees. She laughs about the stories. "I'm kind of a doubter though. I think ghosts aren't in vogue right now. Not as much as alien abductions." She says there haven't been any incidents to report in a long time. The odd customer comes in asking about the ghost stories—mostly writers—but that's the only activity. Last Halloween, the owners celebrated their ten-year anniversary in the location. If there was going to be any sign of Lydia's ghost, or any "weirdness" as Melinda puts it, it seems that would have been the day for it.

The Ghost in the Governor's Mansion

To date, no governor has admitted to seeing a ghost in the gubernatorial estate, but there are former residents who swear the house is haunted.

Millionaire and former Salem mayor Thomas A. Lively built the 10,000 square foot mansion, also known as Mahonia Hall, in 1925. The large Tudor-style home sits on Fairmount Hill overlooking the city. "Hop King" Lively was the largest grower of hops in the state and also vice-president of Oregon Linen Mills. A civic leader, successful farmer and entrepreneur, Lively served as mayor of Salem from 1927 to 1931. As an active Democratic party member, he had the mansion designed for lavish parties with a ballroom on the third floor, a large wine cellar and formal gardens. Although Lively died in 1947 at the age of 84, some say he still presides over events at Mahonia Hall.

A former Salem real estate agent lived in the mansion during the latter part of the 1950s. Neither he nor his wife ever saw a ghost, but they did feel something shaking them out of a deep sleep. They would turn on the lights and the shaking would cease. Strange noises in the kitchen and on the house intercom sounded like birds trapped in the chimney at first. But the scary sounds continued after the chimney was sealed up.

The next owner, W. Gordon Allen, actually saw the image of a man in the master bedroom. During the four years that Allen lived in the home, he received regular visits from a ghost that he believed was the spirit of Thomas Lively. The black-robed man sat on the end of Allen's bed every three or four days, and Allen said the apparition seemed very sad.

In 1988, the home was sold to the state to become the governor's mansion. I contacted the current governor, John Kitzhaber, to see if he and his family had chatted with the original owner. A very pleasant woman from his office got back to me to say she had forwarded my request to the governor. He wanted me to know that neither he, his wife Sharon nor his son Logan had experienced anything one might call ghostly. Previous governors also denied seeing anything out of the ordinary. Could it be their governance has Lively's spectral stamp of approval?

Pittock Mansion

Pioneers Henry and Georgiana Pittock forged a wonderful life together for 58 years. They raised six children and were active and influential in their community. They also built an incredible mansion in which they spent their last years together. Now, several psychics claim the duo continue to monitor Portland's progress. Henry is the more active of the two, and he has sent several messages via various mediums to let everyone know he is still around. The spirits of Henry and Georgiana are not the type, it seems, to rest idly in the afterlife.

Pittock Mansion is the culmination of two lives well lived. Henry Lewis Pittock arrived in Oregon in 1853 by wagon train, having followed the Oregon Trail from Pennsylvania. Without two pennies to rub together, he began working at the *Weekly Oregonian* as a printer's assistant. He started his life on the west coast sleeping on a cot under the newspaper office counter. Before long, he rose through the ranks to take ownership of the *Weekly Oregonian* in 1860. That same year he took a wife, 15-year-old Georgiana Martin Burton of Missouri. Henry Pittock was 25 years old.

In the years that followed, Henry devoted his time to creating an empire. He had his fingers in every pie—real estate, banking, railroads, steamboats, pulp and paper, silver mining and sheep ranching. His wife entrenched herself in the community, working tirelessly to improve the lives of women and children. She helped found the Ladies Relief Society. Its children's home fed and sheltered needy children. She also was integral in the creation of the Martha Washington Home for single working women. In her spare time, Georgiana gardened. Her passion for flowers was the inspiration for Portland's annual Rose Festival.

Extravagant even by today's standards, Portland's Pittock Mansion is still overseen by the ghosts of its original inhabitants.

In 1909, the couple began planning their new home. They hired Edward T. Foulkes, a promising architect, to design a mansion that would eventually overlook Portland. The Pittocks moved into the house in 1914. Everything about it was lavish and progressive. It had a central vacuum system and intercoms. Only the best local materials and Oregon craftsmen had been used to build the house, its three-car garage and greenhouse. Sadly, the couple only lived there for four years. Georgiana died in 1918 at age 73; Henry followed one year later. Perhaps after pouring so much of their heart and soul into the house and the community,

Henry and Georgiana felt unwilling to leave when the time came.

The city saved the house from demolition in the early 1960s. It was restored and turned into a museum in 1965. The ghosts, it seems, remained, eager to greet the public.

Lee is one of three receptionists at the mansion. She told me that on five separate occasions, psychics came to her and told her the same thing—that the house's namesake was still there watching over his home. Lee says the first time it happened she was dumbstruck. "I was sitting at my desk. I looked up and saw this woman who looked like Morticia Addams with long black hair parted down the middle and a long black cape. She threw her cape over her shoulder, leaned down to me and said, 'Mr. Pittock is here in the house, but don't worry. He is very pleased with what you're doing.' And with that she swept out before I could say anything." Lee didn't think too much of it at the time, except that it was an odd thing to happen. But over a two-year period, four other people came forward and used the same words. "That's what I find most unusual, that they used the identical words when they passed on the message." Lee takes small comfort in knowing her ghostly boss is still lurking about. "I don't want to sense him or see him," she says. "I work here late at night sometimes, and I have to lock up the house. I like to think I'm alone here."

What's more, someone or something likes to move a photograph of the young Henry from its place on the bedroom mantel. Lee has heard that it is regularly found lying on the bed that was formerly Mr. Pittock's. Visitors have also reported smelling the strong scent of roses when there were no flowers in the house. Roses, of course, were Georgiana's favorite.

The Dark Side of The Dalles

Vengeful Indian spirits, ghostly gamblers and greedy gold thieves—all are said to haunt various places in the Wasco County area known as The Dalles.

In the push westward, pioneers established the Wascopam Mission in 1838 on what had been a Native American fishing settlement. Twelve years later, the U.S. Army set up Camp Drum on the same site. It came to be known as Fort Dalles, the only military fort on the Oregon Trail between Fort Vancouver and Fort Laramie. In the years that followed, the frontier town that naturally developed around the fort became known as The Dalles.

Stone House

One of the most notorious tales from The Dalles involves Colonel J.H. Neyce, who joined the garrison at Fort Dalles in the early 1860s as a clerk in the quartermaster's office. Soon afterward, he built a massive home for his family to live in. The house was one of startling magnificence for the time. Everything about it was beautiful, dignified and planned for full artistic effect. Sandstone blocks 18 inches thick were quarried from the local bluff, providing the house with its name—Stone House. Sadly, the landmark building did not bring the colonel joy. His young boy died of measles. Neyce's wife died soon after.

While Neyce lived in the house, there were stories of some underhanded financing for the mansion that no one could ever confirm. Though no charges were ever laid, it was implied that Neyce may have bloodied his hands to cover his expenses. Irene Clark wrote in an undated article that Colonel Neyce was known for trying to keep up with his more affluent neighbors, and that his policy seemed to be "Enjoy today. Pay tomorrow—maybe."

The story is that the beaten and burned body of a man was found near a state fairground with only the initials "H.H." tattooed on his breast as identification. On the same day as the murder, a home had been purchased from a man named Henry Hinckley; the buyer paid $1000 cash. The man who bought the home identified the brutalized corpse as that of Hinckley, and said he and others had last seen the dead man in the company of Neyce.

Police never arrested Neyce, but his connection to the murder fueled many stories of foul doings at the colonel's Stone House. Eventually, Neyce fell on hard times and had to give up his huge home. While it was tenantless, dark tales circulated in the community of noises late at night. People imagined hearing the screaming of other victims. Children used to dare each other to run up and ring the doorbell, then run away screaming when a terrible rattling—like someone dragging a heavy chain—was heard within the house. That mystery was solved by a daring boy who stayed behind and discovered the source of the noise was a large Newfoundland dog left chained up by his master while off at work.

Colonel Neyce died at the age of 90 in a California poorhouse. His home burned to the ground in 1905 after the house next door caught fire and high winds carried the flames to Stone House.

Tenth Street House

Residents of a house built on East Tenth Street told a reporter at *The Dalles Chronicle* that they were sure a ghost lived in the basement. Not much is known of the history except that the house was built in 1923 and during Prohibition one owner brazenly sold illegal booze and cigarettes.

The family that lived there until 1996 said they never saw any apparitions but had distinctly creepy feelings whenever they descended the stairs to the basement. The woman said she sensed something lurking in the shadows that gave her goosebumps. She didn't say anything to her husband. He later asked her if she had met the ghost yet. He obviously had experienced the same feelings.

The family confirmed the existence of an unseen presence when they returned from a camping trip. As they entered the stairway to the basement, the dog started barking, its hair bristled and it tucked its tail between its legs. The family moved in 1996 without ever learning if someone had died in the house. They remained sure that a spirit of some kind had shared the space with them.

Fort Dalles Museum

Fort Dalles—or at least what's left of it—stands at the end of the Oregon Trail as a symbol of the bitter, violent clashes between Native Americans and pioneering white men. Could it be that the ghosts of Indians who died in battle continue to circle the fort today?

The Indians were tolerant of the never-ending stream of explorers, trappers, traders and missionaries, but the sudden onslaught of settlers with their wagons, wives, children and plows created tension. The situation disintegrated when disease introduced by the white settlers killed many of the Indians. The Fort Dalles military complex (originally named Camp Drum) was constructed in response to the Whitman Massacre at Walla Walla in 1847. Cayuse Indians slaughtered

The surgeon's quarters at Fort Dalles, one of the oldest museums in Oregon, are rumored to stand on an Indian burial ground

missionaries because they falsely believed that their children had been poisoned after a measles outbreak. The Indians were angry that Dr. Whitman's medicine cured white people but seemed to kill natives—when the problem was actually that the Indians lacked natural immunity.

On March 30, 1850, Colonel William W. Loring established a post at The Dalles. The fort initially consisted of a few leaky frame buildings with dirt floors and open ceilings. The army sent as few men as possible to its only military post between the Pacific Coast and Wyoming. Their job was to patrol the roads and send settlers on their way to the Willamette Valley as quickly as possible.

But the violence worsened. In 1854, gold was discovered near Colville, enticing more people to come to the area. The military captured and killed Indians for atrocities committed against wagon trains. Fort Dalles gained status as the center for treaty negotiations. In 1856, it became headquarters for the Ninth Infantry Regiment, which came to force compliance to the treaties. During that time, new buildings were constructed, including four officer's houses. Colonel George Wright's house cost an impressive $22,000, whereas the more modest surgeon's quarters cost less than $5000.

In the late 1850s, the Indian frontier moved east and the fort no longer served a purpose. A fire caused by faulty mortar in the chimneys razed through the three main houses, burning them to the ground. Only the surgeon's quarters survived. The army kept a caretaker at the fort until the 1880s, after which the few remaining buildings were at the mercy of squatters and the elements. Eventually, the town took over the site, and the museum opened in 1905. Housed in the surgeon's quarters, it is one of Oregon's oldest museums.

The museum's curator told *The Dalles Chronicle* in October 2000 that many visitors believe the surgeon's quarters are haunted. They report feeling a ghostly presence. Some locals believe the fort sits on an Indian graveyard, and children of museum caretakers have reported seeing Indian ghosts stalking them as they played outside.

The McCann House

At least one previous owner claims that one of Bend's historic homes has an extra resident. The three-story house at 440 NW Congress Street was recognized as a national historic site in 1980. It was built in 1916 for Thomas McCann, the first manager of the Shevlin-Hixon Mill in Bend. McCann asked that the home be designed as a mansion, with servants' quarters and sculpted white lions that still stand in front. When Sharron Comeau moved in 60 years later, she says the spirits were there to greet her and her family.

Sharron believes the ghost was the mother of a former owner. The woman apparently died in one of the upstairs bedrooms. Although Sharron sensed a presence in her home, it was her daughter Mary who saw the apparition. Mary slept in the bedroom that had been the woman's. It wasn't long after moving in that Mary told her family there was something odd in one corner of her room. They discovered it was the corner where the woman's bed had been.

The ghost, a misty blue-gray shape of a woman with dark hair, appeared often and would pace in front of the bedroom window wringing her hands. She would even sit on Mary's bed and talk to the teenager. When Mary left for school, her younger sister Amy moved into the room and became acquainted with the friendly spirit.

Over the years, the ghost's visits tapered off. A psychic told Sharron that the woman's spirit was moving on to another level so her presence would be less easy to detect.

10 Windsor Street

There may be something to theories of parallel realities where spirits and humans co-exist. One woman I spoke to had a close encounter that suggests different times and places may overlap.

Kim Olson, who also tells some fascinating stories from her job at Southern Oregon University, lived in a house that sent her running into snowstorms in fear.

"I would be doing homework and would get this overwhelming feeling that if I didn't get out of the house now, I would die," Kim remembers. "It was terrifying—a flight-or-fight response. I would bolt out the front door in my socks. One time it was snowing, and I was sure the neighbors were going to call the police and have me hauled away." Each time, Kim waited for 10 or 15 minutes until the malevolent energy dissipated. She could return to the house only after the shift in energy.

The house at 10 Windsor Street was relatively new when Kim and her family moved in. It was the early 1980s and Kim was in seventh grade. Although the house was only 10 or 15 years old, Kim thinks that some spirit remained connected to the land on which the house was built. Her whole family noticed the strange goings-on. "Things would disappear," she recalls. Kim volunteered as a candy striper (a teenage nurses' aid) at the local hospital, where they had a strict dress code requiring specific nursing shoes. Kim says that on several occasions she would lay out her uniform the night before, and in the morning something would be missing. One day it was her shoes. "They weren't anywhere. We hunted through the whole house. Then one shoe showed up a couple of weeks later in an ironing basket. The other shoe appeared another two weeks later in the back of my dad's closet," Kim explains.

The poltergeist became bolder over time. On one occasion, it took a book that Kim had out of her sight for only a moment. She remembers vividly: "I was reading, of all things, Stephen King's *Pet Cemetery* and had made some tea. I put the book down to pour myself a cup of tea, and when I turned back, the book was gone." She never did get that one back. Perhaps the phantom thief enjoyed the book too much to return it.

Kim's most frightening experience happened one night when she was home alone. She was in her second-floor room when she heard footsteps coming up the stairs from the main floor. Kim froze, thinking she was about to interrupt a burglar. "I thought I was a goner," she recalls.

Terrified, she frantically considered where she might hide until she saw the shadow of an older woman suddenly thrown into relief on the wall. As if cast by someone lit from behind, the shadow revealed the shape of a woman with a severe dowager's hunch, wearing a calf-length dress, a sweater and clunky shoes. Her hair was pulled back into a bun. Kim continues, "As I saw her, she had her hand on the rail and took the last step to the top of the staircase. She turned to look at me and jumped. Then she ran off around the corner to my parent's room." Kim never got over the shadow ghost's reaction. "I always wondered, what if in her world I looked like a ghost to her?" Kim speculates. "Her reaction was so odd, it made me think."

No one else in Kim's family ever saw the shadow woman. They never learned if she was the ghost who took the shoes and book. But Kim believes that the older female spirit was not the same one that caused her to feel threatened and go running from the house.

Kim now lives in a different house with her own family; she says it too seems to have spirits within. She hasn't been able to check the history with the people who sold her the house. Because the previous owners built the house, Kim thinks the spirits are attached to the land rather than the building. "I've heard walking on the stairs and a little child's laughter," she tells me. "My mom has heard that too." Kim says on different occasions both she and her mother have also heard their names called by a young girl. When it happened, they each thought it was Kim's eight-year-old daughter, but when they went downstairs, they found that no one else was in the house.

Some people, Kim acknowledges, seem predisposed or more open to connections with spirits.

Wilcox Mansion

Chandeliers swing by themselves. Pianos play in empty rooms. A woman in a flowing white gown floats between floors in what may have been her home more than a century ago.

For nearly half a century, Wilcox Mansion has been used for business. Portland's KWJJ radio station ran its operation from the manor for 40 years until moving out in April 1997. But the manor's ghostly residents haven't moved out of the opulent three-story home.

The former home of the Theodore B. Wilcox family, Wilcox Mansion was built in 1893 on King Street by the Portland architectural firm of Whidden and Lewis. The same firm designed some of the city's best known buildings, including City Hall and the Multnomah County Courthouse. Wilcox was a millionaire flour miller and grain exporter; with his astute business savvy, he led the way in transforming Portland from a town into a modern city. For his home, Wilcox wanted only the finest materials, so the red sandstone on the exterior of the house was brought from New England. The hand-carved woods inside range from Honduras mahogany to golden oak. Of the seven fireplaces, four are marble, two are brick and one is onyx. Corinthian columns, solid brass fixtures and genuine gold-leaf wallpaper adorn the interior.

The mansion's history suggests that some skeletons still linger in the closet, if not a few ghosts. Wilcox died in 1918 at age 62 after a brief illness. Theodore's wife, Nellie Stevens, lived in the mansion until her death in 1939. Then it was sold. In 1942, it functioned as the headquarters for the Russian Purchasing Commission, and in World War II the Russians operated a school for their children on the premises. The Portland School of Music then moved in and the old walls reverberated with the music of masters such as Rubinstein and Toscannini, who practiced there before concerts. Finally, the radio station, KWJJ-AM, bought it and set up its station.

A former engineer for KWJJ, who requested that his name not be published, worked in the old servants' quarters on the third floor where he spent a lot of time in the large engineering shop. The three other rooms were used for storage. When he began with the company, he told me that people would half-jokingly warn him to watch out for the ghosts up there. "There's no denying it was creepy, especially at night. I always felt someone was watching me."

More to the point, there were a lot of goings-on that the radio engineer could simply not explain. "I would leave the shop and be sure to unplug the soldering irons and turn off the lights. When I came back the lights would be on and the irons plugged in," he recalls. A variety of strange, quirky things would happen sporadically. Coffee cups or tools on a bench would be moved to another part of the shop or knocked to the floor when the engineer left the room. He would routinely close a door upon leaving a room, only to find it open when he came back.

In one room near the engineering shop, there was a wall fixture with a red light bulb that seemed to have a life of its own. It would be off when the man walked by and on the next time he passed. "There's only one way to the third floor and no one would have gone by. I would go and click the light on and off and it would function perfectly. I don't know—it could have been a short, but I don't think so."

The engineer heard many stories wilder than his own. Like any radio station, there were people in the building 24 hours a day. Those on the night shift saw apparitions. Old Mrs. Wilcox apparently died in the master bedroom after spending most of her life in the mansion. People have seen a ghostly figure of a woman in a flowing white gown floating up and down the grand staircase. Some people think it is Mrs. Wilcox, while others believe it is the ghost of a former maid. There are also stories of a dapper old man with white hair who moves about the ground floor and in the attic.

While KWJJ occupied the building, there were two grand pianos, one on the main level and another on the second floor. At night, workers could hear music from the piano on the first floor. When they investigated, no one would be sitting at the bench.

After the radio station moved out, the new owners renovated and leased out the offices to several law firms. I spoke to the receptionist at one firm who heard rumors that a person living in the adjacent apartment building had complained to the mansion's owners. Apparently, someone was watching from a third floor window, even though storage and boxes were the only things up there. The current owner, Peter Greene, however, told me there had been a call, but explained that the person was elderly and perhaps somewhat confused.

Greene himself doesn't know what to make of the ghost stories. During renovations, he spent many long nights working in the house until well after midnight. He never encountered any ghosts or poltergeist activity. He also said none of the new tenants, mostly lawyers, have reported anything strange. The ghosts may be keeping to themselves now that the mood in the building has changed from entertainment to litigation.

5

Spectral Snippets

Griswold School

Helix, in Umatilla County, is home to a school founded by Dr. John Griswold. The school is said to be haunted by both the good doctor and his wife. They can be seen looking in the left window in the gymnasium, although the reports are more often of Dr. Griswold sightings than of his wife.

Sackett Hall, Oregon State University

One of the rooms in Sackett Hall is the site of numerous disturbances, including fires that start inexplicably and objects that move around the room. The rumor is that a girl named Brandy was living in room 121 when she died there one night in the 1950s. Apparently, she had been out with a frat boy who either accidentally or intentionally killed her. Either way, her unhappy spirit still roams the hall as a swirling cloud of dust.

Old Highway 97

There are many accounts of freaky happenings in Oregon's central desert near Culver. Ghosts walk the roads at night. Cows with glowing eyes appear out of nowhere and vehicles travel right through them. The stretch of road is very windy and treacherous. A little over 100 years ago, people were crossing the Crooked River in wagons and stagecoaches. The trail crossing, one mile upstream of the current highway, was an important link between the growing cities in central Oregon. But the narrow wooden bridge could be precarious.

High water would cover the bridge, and icy winter weather made it difficult to climb the steep canyon walls. There were numerous accidents and deaths until the railroad bridge was completed in 1911; it formed a stable transportation link through central Oregon. Even now, there are many car accidents on the stretch of road. Perhaps the drivers are distracted by deadly apparitions?

Fort Stevens State Park

In Astoria's state park, a ghost can be seen and heard making his rounds at night. Or at least his flashlight can be seen. While out walking by the concrete bunkers that once housed two big guns at Battery Russell, witnesses can almost make out the figure of a man behind the bright light. But just before the image becomes clear, the light and whoever was carrying it vanish. Some also say that while walking along the old road, they heard chains clanging as the figure came near.

Linkville Cemetery

This Klamath Falls cemetery should be on Halloween pilgrimages for ghost hounds. The site is more than 150 years old, and it is said to have a grave that glows bright green on every full moon. Strange noises and other odd lights have been seen as well. If there's a full moon scheduled for October 31, it might be worth taking a blanket and camera to watch for the light show.

6

The McMenamins' Paranormal Empire

• • •

Perhaps their Celtic roots instinctively draw Mike and Brian McMenamin to buildings full of spirits. As pioneers of the Pacific Northwest's microbrewing industry, they certainly have done their best to provide refreshment for their human customers. According to their website, the brothers are the fourth largest producers of microbrewed beer in the region. They also own the largest empire of haunted houses, pubs and hotels in the state.

Descendants of James and Ann McMenamin of Ireland's landlocked County Tyrone, Mike and Brian seem to have an appreciation for the hardships endured by their great-great-grandparents. Although the potato fields and famine are far in the past, the brothers carry their family name proudly. They also love historic buildings, and since 1974 they have bought some of Oregon's oldest and most interesting structures, many of which are on the National Register of Historic Places. They make a point of restoring the buildings to their vintage state, keeping many of the original furnishings such as the Olympic Club's Tiffany lamps and pool tables. It's not clear when the pair made the connection between their string of purchases and the otherworldly extras that came included, but they quite enjoy the company of their "spirited" guests.

The White Eagle Tavern is by far the most famous of their haunted establishments, but their first haunted acquisition was the Cornelius Pass Roadhouse. They bought the fine collection of farm buildings in 1986, unaware of the path on which they were about to embark. The Thompson Brewery and Public House and the Edgefield Poorhouse followed four years later. Soon after, they bought the Olympic Club and the

Crystal Ballroom. The White Eagle joined the group in 1998; the Hotel Oregon and the Grand Lodge round out the list. Some of the McMenamins' other properties may also have inexplicable goings-on, but those above are the best documented. Staff historian Tim Hills does a good job of staying on top of the latest light shows and bump-in-the-night encounters. The brothers don't make too much of the ghosts or why they happen to inhabit so many of their properties. Rather than fret, their theory seems to be, "Better have a beer to ponder that concept."

• • •

Cornelius Pass Roadhouse

Recognized as one of the finest collections of rural architecture in Oregon, the Cornelius Pass Roadhouse and associated structures also rank among the state's oldest remaining farm buildings. The granary dates to 1855, the house to 1866 and the rare octagonal barn to 1913. The Hillsboro farmstead is now part of the McMenamins' empire, and the various buildings serve as restaurants, pubs, banquet halls and party rooms (of course, there's also a brewery). For the employees, the past occasionally collides with the present for a little paranormal activity.

Tim Hills, staff historian for McMenamins, explains that the farmstead was established back in the state's infancy and was home to six generations of the Imbrie family. The Imbries arrived from the Kingdom of Fife on the southeast coast of Scotland in the 1840s, part of Oregon's first wave of settlers. As farmers, they immediately set plow to land, carving out their stake in Oregon's fertile soil. By the 1850s, brothers James and Robert had their own farms in Washington

The haunted Cornelius Pass Roadhouse in Hillsboro, formerly home to six generations of the Imbrie family

County. James had developed his acreage in North Plains, and Robert built up his landholdings where the roadhouse now stands. He eventually owned 1500 acres. Robert Imbrie raised the granary in the mid-1850s. Ten years later, his family had swelled to include 12 children, and the original farmhouse could not hold them all. Robert replaced the house with the current three-story, Italian villa-style home.

The house was unchanged for decades, aside from the addition of electricity and running water. The farm evolved as it passed from Robert to his son Frank. Robert's focus was horses and he raised Morgans to sell to local farmers as draft animals. Frank switched to dairy when he inherited the farm, and he built an octagonal barn, the unusual eight-sided structure used for milking and feeding. Frank's son, James, took the farm in yet another direction, shifting to grain and hay production. It was Imbrie barley that provided the vital ingredient for Blitz Weinhard beer. The agrarian tradition ended with James in the 1960s. The house passed to James' third son, Frank, whose children were the sixth and final generation to live there. In 1977, the transformation to food service occurred when Frank's younger brother Gary opened the Imbrie Farmstead Restaurant.

The McMenamins took over the Cornelius Pass Roadhouse in the 1980s when encroaching development threatened the buildings. They purchased the property and began restoring some of the old barns. Until recently, the house continued to function as a restaurant. That's where the reports of ghostly activity have come from. Footsteps have been heard in the attic when only a few employees were left on the premises. Some employees also felt cold spots that were difficult to explain, especially on hot summer days. And there was an odd incident in the attic. A manager went to put some boxes away and found a dead bird lying in the middle of a circle of candles. It appeared to be part of some thrill-seeker's ritual or séance. The owners were not pleased, so the door to the attic is now kept locked.

Over the years, numerous Imbrie family members were born and died in this building. Perhaps their spirits continue to rumble around in the attic.

The roadhouse manager, Christopher, downplays the ghostly activity. After all, a 150-year-old house is bound to make some odd creaks and groans. He admits, however, that there were a few nights that made him think twice. On one occasion, he was the last person out of the building and had made sure all doors and windows were locked before setting the intruder alarm. When he got to his car and looked back, the lights were on. Yet no one reported the lights as being on the next morning. Christopher didn't investigate, so he still has no explanation for what might have caused the lights to switch on.

A former employee found herself feeling very uncomfortable one night when she was alone on the second floor. She was vacuuming and noticed that the trapdoor to the attic was open. Turning off the vacuum, she went over to the door and latched it firmly shut. She returned to her cleaning. A few minutes later she glanced over at the door and was shocked to see it wide open again. She unplugged the vacuum and hightailed it downstairs.

The old Victorian house is no longer a restaurant, but it is used for special events. A new barn-style pub, Imbrie Hall, opened in May 2001 to replace the roadhouse. Christopher says that although the new restaurant is made from recycled wood, "it doesn't seem to have imported any spirits."

The Edgefield Poorhouse

Edgefield is known as the mother of all the McMenamins' haunts. The two brothers own several old properties with well-known histories, but Edgefield in Troutdale has ghost stories galore. How could it be otherwise with such an intriguing history? It was a farm for poor people and a nursing home for most of its years, so it was also the scene of many "departures" from this earthly realm. It appears, however, that some of the former residents didn't venture too far.

Edgefield is a complex of several buildings that used to be the Multnomah County Poor Farm. It was built in 1911, before the days of social welfare programs, to house the elderly, disabled, mentally challenged and infirm, along with the poor. Although many such establishments were horrific environments, Edgefield was so prosperous and well managed that its fields not only fed its inmates but generated an excess that was sold to make a profit. In 1947, the facility changed to become a nursing home. It eventually closed in 1982. After several vacant years, it was bought by the McMenamins, who began refurbishing each of the buildings.

The Ad House, as it is known, used to be the poor farm's administrative building. For 70 years or so it housed the superintendent and his family. It now serves as a bed and breakfast. Don't be surprised if you stay there and find yourself being awakened by a female figure at the foot of the bed, shaking your feet. Tim Hills, keeper of the McMenamins' ghost lore, tells me that it is the habit of the female ghost there to shake the feet of sleeping guests. For the most part, she resides in the Althea Room on the top floor of the house. She has also been heard serenading guests with nursery rhymes.

Although the Edgefield Poorhouse has witnessed many departures from this world, some of its spirits appear reluctant to leave.

Originally the farm's power plant and laundry, the power station now functions as a restaurant. Although the spirits there are not as physical or visible as the young woman in the Ad House, staff members often say they feel a presence in the room watching them.

Jeff Bryant has heard all the stories, but in his eight years as manager at Edgefield, he says there was only one time when he was freaked out. In room 215, one of the most notoriously haunted rooms in the complex, he says, "I got some extremely weird vibes." The room was completely covered with graffiti when the McMenamins took over. It seemed to have been used by cultists, because a pentagram was painted on the floor. Some guests report that the spirit of a large dog lives in the room, and there have been complaints that the spirit dog shoves its cold nose in their faces while they are sleeping.

Recently, Jeff heard that two employees looked out the window at around 2 AM and saw an older woman dressed in white gazing in. One of those who reported this sight was the night auditor, who was quite clear about what she saw. A pub worker saw the same thing and also witnessed a young child dressed in white wandering out toward the parking lot. It is believed that the little girl is the spirit of a former caretaker's daughter who died on the property. A psychic medium who stayed at Edgefield confirmed that a young person's energy exists there.

Although much of the lore is often corroborated by guests, Jeff claims that some of the stories are blatantly fictional. He says one such fable involves a gnome-like creature jumping around the wine barrels in the basement. Jeff maintains that this account simply doesn't correspond with the stories of older people dressed in white.

There have also been guests who called down to the front desk to say they could hear someone crying. A few people have asked if there is a daycare on the premises, because they hear the sounds of children crying. Jeff says those spirits may hearken back to the 1960s when part of the complex was used to house troubled children. Coincidentally, one wing that now has lodging rooms used to be the infirmary.

"A lot of people did pass away here," acknowledges Jeff. "That's a fact." After a few nights at Edgefield, even skeptics

tend to be convinced that some of those former residents
have not yet checked out. Maybe there is something to the
old adage my grandfather used to repeat: "If you're not careful, you'll end up in the poorhouse." He neglected to add that
if you're really unlucky, you could end up there forever!

Hotel Oregon

Although a ghost named John is well known at this historic
hotel, no one has any idea who he was in mortal form. He
started showing up in the 1980s and since then has amused
local shopkeepers, hotel employees and customers alike with
his tricks and shenanigans.

The Hotel Oregon in McMinnville is hard to miss—at
four stories, it stands as the tallest commercial building in
Yamhill County. Founded in 1843 as one of the four original
Oregon counties, Yamhill County lies at the northern end of
the Willamette Valley. Its 718 square miles contain lush farm-
land, fine wineries and a rich historical heritage.

The Hotel Oregon's history dates back to 1905, when local
farmer and restaurateur Thomas A. White opened its doors
as the Hotel Elberton. "The best and most up-to-date hotel
west of Portland," was the billing for the hotel then. It offered
a wide range of modern amenities, such as a banquet hall, 26
guest rooms, a ladies' parlor and a street-level barber shop.
McMinnville's two other hostelries simply could not compete. In 1910, White added the third and fourth floors,
though he never finished the fourth level.

In the 1920s, the hotel was a popular stop for traveling
vaudeville companies and sales agents. The Elberton Grill,
the hotel's restaurant, became the hot place to hang out for
the students at Linfield College.

A benevolent ghost named John haunts the Hotel Oregon in McMinnville.

After Thomas White's death in 1932, Arnold "Nick" Nicolai bought the hotel and undertook the next wave of upgrades. The hotel got a makeover, with a more modern interior, more storefronts and an elevator. Nick also renamed it the Hotel Oregon. It enjoyed a booming wartime business, especially with the 1933 repeal of Prohibition. When World War II ended, business spiked upward. The Greyhound bus depot moved in and the Paragon Room opened, both of which substantially built up the clientele. The hotel lobby doubled as the bus waiting area. A soda fountain, snack bar, bookstore and Western Union office were soon added to cater to the transit crowd.

The slide into silence began in the late 1950s. The Paragon Room, with its Naughahyde booths and neon lights, closed. In 1967, the hotel water pipes burst during a frigid winter. The guest rooms had to be vacated and the hotel business closed. In 1975, the bus station moved out. The snack counter closed. Beauty Maid rolled up the carpet. Things became very quiet. It was during this time that reports of ghostly activity started to surface. The entity made its first appearances in and around the street-level storefronts. Shopkeepers felt things like chills and gusts of wind. Objects would inexplicably fall off shelves, as if an unseen hand had given a helping flick. No one knew who the ghost was, so the retailers dubbed him "John."

Meanwhile, the historic property caught the eye of brothers Mike and Brian McMenamin, and they eventually bought it. By 1998, the renovation and restoration was complete, and the upper three stories of the hotel reopened. John is not a malevolent ghost. He mostly wanders closely behind people. Guests or cleaning staff say they feel a presence behind them, but no one is ever there when they turn to look. Tim Hills says John seems more like Casper than a scary ghost. He swings on doors and occasionally has thrown things across the room, but generally in a playful way.

Manager Kris Haley-Eggers says she hasn't seen anything out of the ordinary in quite a while. Maybe all the restoration will set his spirit at ease, and John will get himself a cosmic bus ticket out of town.

The Grand Lodge

Whether manifesting themselves in the scent of lilac or in the sound of children's laughter, the spirits of the past wander freely through the aptly named lodge. In fact, the inexplicable activity has been so frequent and impressive that front desk staff at the Grand Lodge even keep a "ghost log" to keep track of the numerous guest and employee experiences. I am extremely grateful to Lindsay at the lodge's front desk, who graciously provided me with some examples of the comments people have written.

Within weeks of the lodge's opening, guests were recording comments like the following: "Table #18 is haunted!! Apparently by a finicky waitress. On March 21, while preparing to eat our meal, my husband used a squeeze bottle of Grey Poupon mustard on his hamburger. When he placed the mustard back onto the table, it rose slightly and turned 90 degrees as if someone had picked it up and turned it back around. Spooky, huh?"

The beautiful brick-and-column main building was originally built on 13 pastoral acres in Forest Grove as "a pleasant haven from the stress, turmoil and the storms of life's voyage." When it opened in 1922, the lodge was known as the Masonic and Eastern Star Home, and it provided a dignified and comfortable home for the Masonic Temple's aged and infirm freemasons. The home relocated to a new facility in 1999, and the McMenamins became caretakers of the regal establishment. It opened for business March 1, 2000.

In 1926, a smaller building called the Children's Cottage opened to house the orphans of freemasons. The idea didn't last long. It seems the elderly and the children were like oil and water. In 1931, the last orphans were relocated to other families or homes. Now the building has five meeting rooms and the lodge administration offices. It also seems to have its fair share of paranormal sounds and sights. That's where I tracked down one of the sales staff, Debbie, who told me a few of her and her colleagues' experiences.

"The biggest story happened last summer," recalls Debbie. One of the youngest of four sisters who had lived in the house came to visit. The woman, Leah, is now in her mid-to-late 70s. She was accompanied by her son and found the visit very hard as she relived a difficult time in her childhood. The children were cared for, but they had to work hard in the kitchens in the main lodge. They did not have an easy life there. Leah and her three sisters were among the last to leave the cottage in 1931, and four of the meeting rooms are named after them. Leah identified a picture of herself on the wall when she was about three years old. She took Debbie on a tour of the building, remembering things that happened along the way. "She was telling us stories that sent goosebumps down my arms," says Debbie. "When she was a little girl, she would go down in the basement with her playmates." Leah told Debbie that no one else would have known that the kids played down there, but then Debbie remembered a chilling fact. She explains: "Our maintenance man has an office down there and he told us that before Leah's visit he often heard the sounds of children playing and laughing. Suddenly it made sense."

Employees and guests have heard the sounds of children running in the upstairs hall. But Debbie says it was a one-on-one encounter between a former site manager and a ghost that frightened a few of the sales staff. The woman was using the upstairs washroom when she distinctly heard a little girl's voice ask her, "What are you doing?" The space had originally been part of a girl's dormitory. The question sent the woman

The Grand Lodge in Forest Grove, once a home for elderly freemasons

scurrying downstairs; she refused to go up there again. As far
as they know, nothing bad ever happened in the building, so
the administrative staff often wonder who the little children
are and why they can hear their voices.

Debbie says she hasn't seen or heard anything herself, but
she has felt her neck hairs rise while she was on the second
floor. "I had to go there to decorate for Christmas, and I felt
like someone was watching me. It was very creepy. I know
this seems crazy, but I asked that I never be required to go
there alone again." She admits that the power of suggestion
may be the real cause of the feeling, but nonetheless keeps to
the main floor when she is by herself.

Over in the main lodge, there are several stories from
guests who sensed a presence in their room. One ghost is a

woman who wears a pungent lilac perfume. Apparently, the scent was strong enough to drive at least one guest from the room.

Monique Martinsen writes in the ghost log of her meeting with an elderly female ghost in room 228 in October 2000. "I went upstairs to our room to leave my 'save-for-later' box [of food left over from dinner]. I was looking forward to rejoining my husband downstairs for a ghost walk." As Monique walked through the hall to her room, she consciously welcomed any spirits who might be around. Her open, aware state may be responsible for what happened next. She continues: "In our room, I sensed immediately a little old lady, 'Ginny' or 'Virginia.' But then I dismissed it, figuring I was trying too hard. I put my food box on the night table by the bed and half seriously said out loud, 'Well Ginny or Virginia, you are welcome to my dinner if you'd like some.'"

Monique looked away for a second, and when she looked back, a pile of her napkins had been symmetrically arranged next to the box. "No way I had done it!" avows Monique. She got the feeling that the old woman was there with her. She ran to find her husband but couldn't locate him. When she returned, "the box had been perfectly lined up and the little plastic fork and spoon that I had laid aside were perfectly lined up on their upright edges (not flat). The fork lay next to the salad and the spoon next to the stew, both on their edges! Inside the opened box!" Monique says that she got a very pleasant feeling from the woman's presence in her room—a sense of "Don't worry."

A guest in room 224 writes of her August 27, 2001, stay: "I was sleeping and having some dreams that were different than usual. I woke up with a start and saw a ghostly being

A "ghost log" for guests at the renovated Grand Lodge contains many accounts of the paranormal.

floating in the room. I also saw something run across the luggage rack, and [I] hollered at my husband to turn the light on. By the time he did, it was gone."

In room 220, Heidi writes, "I was just returning from the restroom at 4:30 AM; I got back in bed (top bunk) and was just getting ready to go back to sleep when this strong energy force shot through my entire body, from my toes to the top of my head. It happened three or four times. I tried to call out, but my mouth was paralyzed, and I could not move. It honestly felt like somebody or something was running through my body. I did not see a thing, but [it] was definitely there, only in my body. Pretty scary. The funny thing is, I told them (in my head) to stop playing around with me, and they immediately stopped."

Employees at the lodge have made entries as well. Mary Jones, one of the cleaning staff, writes about one experience while cleaning up the bar in one of the rooms. "As I was about to exit, I felt a blast of cold air over my body. I approached the window to close it, and it was already closed. So I looked at the ceiling for some sort of vent and there wasn't one. I then proceeded to close the door, and for some reason there was a pressure on the door as if it wanted to stay open. I finally locked the door, stepped back and noticed the lights on the chandelier flicker. Someone wanted out—now to find out who."

In another incident, a front desk clerk stuck with the Christmas Eve shift in 2001 found that she was not entirely alone. "The restaurant was closed and everyone [the other staff] had gone home. All of the guests were tucked away in their rooms. Everything was very quiet. Then about ten o'clock (maybe 10:30) I heard the unmistakable sound of a glass tipping over in the main bar. Being the curious type (and wondering if it was a mischievous guest), I went to look in the bar. No guests, no tipped-over glass. Satisfied, I proceeded back to the desk. Not five seconds after sitting down, *tink*, that same sound. By now I was fairly creeped out. Nervously I approached the bar again—still nothing. I tried to ignore the sounds. It wasn't until I went down into the basement that I really got scared. It was a cold, creepy feeling—I don't really know how to explain it. All I can say is I raced back up to the desk and didn't move the rest of the night. Merry Christmas!"

Another story, which made local headlines, involved tile artist Jeanne Ralston, who was working on a project for the establishment. She had her own room in which she locked all her tools and equipment. In her ghost log entry, which follows Monique's, Jeanne writes, "I don't know. You might want to worry a bit. I've been working out here off and on for over a year doing tile work in the basement, during which time I've had a couple of weird vibes, but nothing significant. Nothing until today."

On that day, she opened the door to the storage room she had been using and found that someone had been there overnight. "The first thing I noticed was that the broken rock that I left spread out on my scaffold was stacked into two piles, very intricately balanced. My hammer was standing on end on the top of the mastic bucket, my cord was hanging on the end of the scaffold, my tile nippers were hooked in my utility lamp. All of which were lying in disarray when I turned off the light and shut the door (which automatically locks) yesterday evening. At this point I immediately ran upstairs in search of witnesses. When I returned with Hadley, one of the people working out here, we saw the word 'LEAVE' spelled out in tiny chips of rock. I suppose it's possible that someone was pranking me," writes Jeanne. "But no keys to that room were checked out. Creepy."

Jeanne adds, "On a side note, I'm not entirely sure that someone didn't tuck me in last night. I woke up around 4 AM and the sheet and blanket that I had pulled down to get into bed were tightly tucked under the mattress. Maybe it was the nice lady from the previous story [Virginia] trying to make up for the jerk who was busy attempting to freak me out in the basement."

Maybe one of those former masons would rather be doing the tile job himself?

The Crystal Ballroom

It's been a special place in Portland for nearly nine decades—a dancehall like no other. With musical guests such as the Dancing Valentinos, Jerry Garcia and Bo Diddley, the Crystal Ballroom holds memories of "first loves, police raids, hallucinogenic visions, visits by smoldering screen stars and Beat poets, narrow escapes from fire, demolition and neglect, and a listing in the National Register of Historic Places." So writes McMenamins historian Tim Hills on a website entitled *The Many Lives of the Crystal Ballroom*.

Tim also tells me that the dance and music hall could still send a shiver up one's spine for spectral reasons. It seems some performers or guests of the past may have found the place too exciting to leave. Maybe, as Tim suggests, it's Rudolph Valentino back for a return engagement. Footsteps and laughter have been heard upstairs in the ballroom when the building was locked up and no one was supposed to be there.

Right from the start, the building that eventually became the Crystal Ballroom set itself apart from normal buildings. In 1873, Captain John H. Couch divided his property into smaller parcels, choosing to orient this particular lot with the Willamette River instead of the streets of Portland. The result was the creation of an irregular city block, with the property

The elegant Crystal Ballroom in Portland, complete with "floating" dance floor

in question wedged between two normal lots. The shape affected the building's design, but not its ultimate popularity.

There were a few obstacles to overcome along the way. When the ballroom, originally named Cotillion Hall, opened in 1914, Portland's chief moral crusader and suffragette, Lola Baldwin, warned, "Dance the tango and you face arrest." However, owner Montrose Ringler stood firm against such opponents in his desire to run a respectable dancehall.

He drew people in with an unusual "floating" dance floor. The floor is something special. It is the kind of thing that has to be experienced to be believed, mainly because it bounces. It is the remarkable invention of Charles R. Hunt of Sacramento, California. Hunt ingeniously devised the mechanical floor, which he created by layering wood planks on top of 800 rocker panels (like the kind in rocking chairs) that had ball bearings attached to each end. The whole floor would sway when people danced on it, and the rocking motion could be controlled with a set of ratchet gears to increase or decrease the motion, depending on the type of dance. Hunt's idea was to reduce the stress and fatigue for dancers. It seemed to work. Dancers said it was "like dancing on a cloud." It remains distinctive, and it is thought to be the only floor like it in the United States.

Ringler and his partner, Paul Van Fridagh, successfully defied the anti-dance movement. Nevertheless, in 1921 Ringler left the business and Van Fridagh died in 1925. After that, the hall slid into neglect and disrepair. For a while it was home to the local African-American community, offering some of the city's first public black dances. Eventually, the rock and roll era took over. The building reopened as the Crystal Ballroom in 1950, featuring jazz music and names such as James Brown and Marvin Gaye. But increasing competition with big-name bands in better spaces eventually spelled financial disaster. The Crystal Ballroom closed in 1968 and remained a vacant landmark until the McMenamins bought it in 1997. In reopening it, they may have disturbed the spirits of entertainers or patrons who had been enjoying a ghostly turn on the dance floor.

Current manager Clyde Fulkerson says there hasn't been much to report since he joined the team. People talk about hearing things, but most of it is hearsay. However, previous employees reported seeing people when the building was supposed to be empty.

There's an account in Jefferson Davis' *Ghosts, Critters and Sacred Places of Washington and Oregon* of one night in 1998 when the burglar alarms went off and the security company summoned the manager. He arrived alone and walked through the building, including the ballroom, only to find no one around and nothing disturbed. He was on the floor below the ballroom, about to enter his office, when he suddenly heard several loud voices and the footsteps of a group of people at the top of the stairs. The voices and steps got fainter as the group walked across the ballroom. The manager realized it was unlikely any human group could have evaded his search (they would probably not be so bold), so he decided not to investigate any further and let the voices disappear.

The Olympic Club

This story takes place a little outside Oregon's borders in Centralia, Washington. The place is owned by the McMenamin brothers, who seem to have more than half a dozen haunts in their empire.

Manager Joel Wall says there are plenty of strange things that occur at the Olympic Club. Are the staff, for example, hearing the ghostly footsteps of one of the loggers whose spiked boots once marked the floor? Or is it the man they have named "Elmer," who died during a fire? Joel's not sure, but he knows there are definitely spirits of some sort roaming through the grand relic.

The Olympic Club was billed as a "gentlemen's resort" when it opened its doors to loggers, miners and railroad workers in 1908. Given the grim conditions of laborers during the time, the place was paradise. The men, many of whom were poor immigrants, worked ten-hour days, six days a week, for a couple of dollars a day. They toiled in extremely dangerous environments where fatal accidents occurred regularly. There was little joy in their lives. Worse, the laborers lived in primitive, unhealthy shacks with little heat and lots of vermin. With its opulent decor and entertainment, the Olympic Club offered the men a measure of dignity and a much-needed respite from their backbreaking labor.

The saloon also had a darker, rowdy side. It was *the* bootlegging center for the area, and although the owners were always getting arrested, they were never convicted. The hotel next door was actually a brothel. Then there was the event that came to be known as the Centralia Massacre of 1919. The labor union was pushing to improve the abysmal working conditions, and it went head-to-head with the mill owners,

Stories about Elmer, the Olympic Club's mischievous spirit, seem to revolve around fire and bagpipe music.

quickly making enemies in the town. During an Armistice Day parade after World War I, the anger and frustration boiled over into the streets. The mill owners rushed the union hall, only to find the labor members armed and ready to fight. There were several deaths, injuries and arrests. Since the Olympic Club was the town's central gathering place, most of the customers knew of the union's plan. At the same time, the owners of the club were privy to the city's strategy. It made for plenty of intrigue within the club's walls.

Since then, the club has been restored as a restaurant and bar, with the original Tiffany lamps and pool tables. Perhaps not surprisingly, many unexplainable things happen there.

Joel says the interesting thing is that most of the strange incidents involve fire—a fire alarm goes off, the stove door opens, extinguished candles suddenly ignite. The consensus is that the events are tied to a fire that burned down the wood-framed hotel next door in 1908. An immigrant butcher, whom Joel and his staff called "Elmer," lived upstairs in the hotel, and when the fire broke out he couldn't get down.

In fact, Elmer's real name may have been Louis Galba. According to Tim Hills' research, Galba arrived in Centralia early in the 20th century. A former Chicago stockyard worker, he eventually became a first-rate butcher. He worked at a local meat shop and lived above the Star Saloon. On June 26, 1908, the saloon went up in flames. Trapped upstairs, unable to escape the inferno, Galba jumped out the back window of his second-story room to avoid the fire. He suffered such severe injuries in the fall that he died three months later. Galba, now called Elmer, might be the ghost who is haunting the club.

"One thing that happened to me personally involves the huge wood stove," Joel tells me over the phone. "It is lit every day except in the summer. It's always out by the time I get here in the morning. Usually I come in, turn on the lights, check around, then go light the fire." One morning as Joel was going through his routine, he noticed that the fire was out, the stove was cold and there were two pieces of wood left unburned. "After doing a few things I turned and could see fire through the stove door. I went to look and sure enough, those logs were flaming. They had been dead out. It was so weird." Joel figured it must be Elmer up to his old tricks.

Another common occurrence is candles that simply won't go out. He says that the restaurant uses liquid fuel cell candles that last a certain number of hours before running out. By the end of the night, the candles are usually out. "When they are still burning in the morning, it's creepy," says Joel. "A lot of times we see candles still lit, and just out of curiosity I'll call the night manager and ask if they did a walk through to make sure all the lights and candles were out. They say yes, but we come in to find lights on and candles burning. I might think it was just them not being thorough, but it happens so often, it makes you wonder."

People often report feeling someone brushing by them or hearing footsteps upstairs toward the back end of the house. Former manager Chad Cooper noticed that most of Elmer's appearances coincided with performances by the club's piper. The sound of bagpipes obviously awakened something in the ghost. On the evenings when the piper played, employees caught glimpses Elmer in front of the hot stove.

One other major incident made believers of many skeptics. Several years ago, the assistant manager was closing the restaurant one night. Two other people were with her, and they were discussing Elmer. One person vehemently denied the possibility that there was a paranormal presence on the premises. Just then, the fire alarm went off for no reason. They rushed to the panel in the wall and tried to get it to turn off, but it wouldn't. The keypad was unresponsive. The disbeliever shouted out, "I'm sorry, Elmer!" and the alarm immediately stopped ringing. All three people involved were "freaked out," according to Joel.

"Those are the main things that have made us aware that this is a little bit more than myth," Joel says. Now the staff advertise that the club has a resident ghost. "Overall, he's a friendly fire prankster," adds Joel. To this day, there are still customers who, having no idea about the history of the building, ask if the club has a ghost or comment that they feel a presence from time past. Maybe Elmer just likes to heat things up a little.

The White Eagle

A popular watering hole on Russell Street in North Portland, the White Eagle has to be one of Oregon's most famous haunts. Every Halloween, ghost hunters, the media and enthusiasts of the otherworldly make pilgrimages to the White Eagle. They come with their cameras and tape recorders, hoping for a glimpse of Sam the cook, Rose the prostitute and the Chinese bouncer—the bar's paranormal celebrities whose stories are known worldwide. People want to hear about the brothel upstairs and the shanghai tunnel downstairs. Is there any truth to it all? Unfortunately, the line between fact and fiction has become quite blurred. But ask anyone—there's no doubt that at least one ghostly resident lives in the pub.

Much of the strange activity happens on the second floor and in the basement. Objects are tossed out of nowhere, people feel groping, invisible hands push people and old coins materialize on the floor. The washrooms seem replete with apparitions. An invisible presence enters the men's room and flushes the toilet. Phantoms in the women's washroom have locked stall doors. The sound of a woman crying is heard on the second floor.

Psychics who have examined the tavern say that the various presences are sometimes overwhelming. They consistently report a sensation of violence and death in the basement, some playful and mischievous energy on the main floor and a deep well of sadness on the second floor. This assessment seems in keeping with the legends that surround the old saloon.

The Russell Street landmark began serving beers back in 1906. It was part of the rough, working-class neighborhood of Lower Albina on the waterfront, and the clientele were often recent arrivals from Europe, Russia, the Balkans and Asia. As the docks, factories and mills emptied at day's end, exhausted men would walk to the Eagle for a pint before heading home.

Polish immigrants William Hryszko and Bronislaw "Barney" Soboleski opened the White Eagle to help out their recently arrived countrymen. In fact, the name is a reference to the symbol on the Polish flag. While the suds flowed on the main floor, the second story became a meeting hall for the politically oriented Polish National Alliance. In fact, the meetings held there contributed to a dirty little part of Portland's history—U.S. Secret Service agents falsely arrested seven PNA members as anarchists in a raid that turned up pamphlets filled with patriotic hymns rather than anti-government propaganda.

While Hryszko and Soboleski offered pool, poker and liquor on the main floor, customers with the right connections and enough money, it was said, could gain entry to the brothel on the second floor or the opium den in the basement. The basement was notorious for having a tunnel that connected to an underground network leading to the waterfront. It was said that unlucky or drunk patrons were shanghaied through the passageway to fill the ranks of ships' crews.

The legends also claimed that white prostitutes worked upstairs, while the basement was home to the black courtesans. A muscle-bound Chinese bouncer was apparently hired to keep the peace between the two groups of customers, but one night he mysteriously disappeared, never to be seen again.

As for Rose and Sam, there are a few variations on who they were. Rose was supposed to be a teenage prostitute who worked in the brothel. Sam is known to have been a real person, though the details of his past have been distorted over time. One account has it that Sam was a ten-year-old street urchin who was taken in by one of the owners. He apparently worked as a housekeeper to earn his room and board, and died in the 1930s at the age of 30 in his second-floor room. Other stories have it that Sam was Rose's lover, and that he killed her. And yet another version says Sam died alone in his room in his sixties, a victim of alcoholism.

In fact, Sam Worek was an Old World immigrant who became a close friend of the Hryszko's. According to his naturalization papers, he was born in 1885 in a Polish enclave in Austria and immigrated to the United States in 1905. Sam's journey took him west to Portland, and he moved into the White Eagle in 1910 to become the very popular resident cook. Apparently Sam liked to drink, and it resulted in long absences when he was on binges. But he always came back to his room on the second floor and his job in the kitchen. As for his death, Sam was not murdered but grew old; most stories say he did not die at the White Eagle. He lived to be 70 and died in Salem. The clothes and other belongings found in his old room belonged to someone else. So either the ghost that everyone thinks is Sam is actually that of another wayward spirit, or perhaps Sam came back to the place he knew best and where he lived most of his life.

The colorful ghosts of Portland's White Eagle reflect the bar's working-class history.

Historian Tim Hills dug into the other stories and found there is little evidence to support the brothel or opium den legends. There are many inconsistencies between them and the historical facts. For example, the era of shanghais had passed when the tavern opened. And although tunnels did exist in the city, they were in the west end where most of the Asian community resided. Those families did build underground networks, but they didn't extend to Albina. A place in the basement may have fueled the rumors because it looks like the start of a tunnel, but it was really the old coal chute. Hills says the truth of the White Eagle's history is a lot less glamorous. The laborers in the upstairs rooming house may have brought women back to their rooms now and then, but it wasn't a brothel. Police records of the time show, in fact, that Albina had a relatively low crime rate. Most of the activity in the building was related to the practical meetings of the Polish community. But that doesn't explain the strange goings-on that are regularly documented.

Chuck Hughes owned the saloon for about 20 years before the McMenamins bought it in 1998. Hughes firmly believed in the ghosts there. In *Ghosts and Strange Critters of Washington and Oregon*, Jefferson Davis writes that Chuck Hughes was working late one night in his basement office when he heard a coin drop on the bar floor above him and roll across the wood. He ran up to see who was still there but found the bar empty. He returned to his office, and a few minutes later he heard the coin drop and roll again. This time he also heard footsteps follow the runaway coin. That was enough to chase Hughes out of the building. He also reported that he would often return to find the lights turned off, although he made a point of leaving the bar lights on so police making rounds could easily check the interior.

The Chinese bouncer is said to frequent the stairway. It seems he pushes women from behind, and employees often feel a shove while going up or down the stairs. One day, Chuck heard one of his waitresses scream. He rushed to find the woman, who claimed to have psychic abilities, at the bottom of the stairs. She claimed that she had been picked up by her shirt and carried to the bottom of the stairwell.

The McMenamins' employees say that such supernatural events continued after the White Eagle changed ownership. Current manager John McBarren says it's been fairly quiet lately. But there are several incidents that people still talk about. One kitchen employee looked up once to see a dry-erase board fly across the room, hit the wall and slide down the stairs to the basement.

John relates another event in the bar that spooked both patrons and employees. It was late afternoon on a Sunday. The band hired for the day had just finished its set and people were gathering their coats and streaming out. One of the customers suddenly said loudly, "Look at that!" She was pointing to the old hard hat that sits on top of the bar as a reminder of the bar's roots. The hat was upside down and spinning. Then, as John puts it, "it flung itself off the bar and landed at this woman's feet."

The incidents are endless. One bartender felt someone flicking the back of his head while he was serving drinks. A door that suddenly unlatched and swung open hit another employee carrying supplies into the large walk-in freezer in the basement. Delivery people have reported feeling a cold hand on the back of the neck while depositing boxes in the basement.

Upstairs in the hotel, there have also been strange events. John McBarren says the second floor was distinctly creepy before the renovations were completed in October 2000. The floor had been very dark. All the lights had tarpaper covers, and everyone felt the pervasive sadness. Visiting psychics would feel a "whoosh" of melancholy every time the door to the upper floor was opened.

Some paranormal experts distinguish ghosts from spirits—they say that spirits can communicate with the living, but that ghosts can't. If someone frequents a place where a deceased person spent much of his or her time, it is not uncommon for the flesh-and-blood person to experience a form of psychic communication with the entity. Sudden and unexplained feelings of sadness or melancholy are common indications, especially if restricted to one particular room or area.

Shortly after the hotel opened, the parents of an employee staying upstairs had an unexpected night visitor. The mother woke up in the middle of the night and saw a man wearing a nightshirt and holding a lamp standing at the foot of her bed. She roused her husband, but by the time he awoke, the apparition had disappeared.

John McBarren is a pragmatist: "I think a lot of it is suggestion. I think the feelings are really there, but what they mean is open to interpretation. The sadness could be from the lonely workers who missed their families." He suggests that the people who bought the tavern from the original owners about 30 years ago made up a lot of the stories, because that's when they began to circulate. It would have been good for business to create a little intrigue. John says relatives of founder William Hryszko are actually upset by some of the legends because they denigrate the family name.

Still, McBarren admits the Eagle is "kind of creepy" when he's there alone late at night. He speculates that because the business is one of the last in the city that still does what it did nearly a hundred years ago, it may still serve as a meeting place for ghosts who don't recognize any of the new developments in the area.

Thompson Brewery and Public House

Whether it's the ghost of the first resident of the old Victorian house, Franklin Thompson, or Ludwig, the Crown Prince of Bavaria, no one knows for sure. But employees at the Thompson Brewery and Public House in South Salem are certain that some spirit has been having mischievous fun moving things around and making odd sounds.

Franklin Thompson and his wife moved into the intriguing hilltop home in 1905. Thompson had fought for the North in the Civil War, and the house, with its orchard-covered rolling hills, was a perfect place to retire in peace. After the Thompsons died, the house was occupied by various businesses, including a real estate firm, an interior design shop, a preschool and a beauty salon. In 1990, the McMenamin brothers transformed it into the first brewpub in Salem since Prohibition.

Steve Hedenskog manages the Thompson Brewery. He started there shortly after it opened, and he says he hasn't seen anything unusual. He's there by himself often, either to open or close the pub, and if there is a ghost, it hasn't bothered to make Steve's acquaintance. Other staff members, however, have had some fairly unusual experiences.

Sue joined Thompson's six months after it opened. She and her co-workers joked about the ghost, who they nicknamed Franklin, but she was skeptical "until one night there was a specific incident that was a turning point for myself and my co-worker, Becky," explains Sue. That evening, they had turned everything off and sat down to write in the restaurant logbook. Both women heard footsteps upstairs, and in the dim, after-hours light they joked around to scare each other. But a couple of minutes later, just a few feet away, they heard a clicking sound. "Then we heard a loud beep," Sue recalls. "We couldn't directly see the register, because there was a partition in the way, but it sounded like the register going on. We went to check, and sure enough it was on, but the key was turned off. There's no way that it could have been on with the key in the 'off' position." Sue and Becky then noticed the coffee pot light was also on. That really did scare them, and they hightailed it out of there.

"I still hadn't seen anything, but I knew for sure that there was something in the pub. No one could have been joking or playing a prank on us. There was no doubt in my mind after that," Sue adds.

Soon afterward, Sue and Becky got visual confirmation of their ghost. One night, Sue was helping out on the second floor where the tables are in separate rooms and alcoves. A short, brown-haired gentleman wearing a brown sweater walked past Sue into a little side room. Becky told him someone would be with him soon. When Sue went to check on him, the room was empty. "We both saw him. We went downstairs and checked the whole place. No one fit his description. I even waited outside the men's restroom to see if he'd come out."

That was the beginning of what Sue and Becky call "the sightings." In fact, several of the eight workers saw the ghost. There was a beer storage shed out behind the house, and Sue said she caught countless glimpses of him there. "He was a prankster," she explains. "We weren't scared of him after a while. He'd be there, egging me on to come out. I would only see half of him, like he was hiding half behind, and he would beckon with his finger to come over."

Sue remembers that customers would walk in the door and ask if there was a ghost there. That always surprised her. Franklin's great-grandchildren lived in the area, and they used to visit the pub. When Sue told them of her encounters, they told her, "Oh yeah, that sounds like Grandpa Frank."

Customers and staff also felt extremely cold chills in various parts of the house. One employee felt a gush of cold air in the Ludwig Room, where the bust of Ludwig, Crown Prince of Bavaria, still sits. All the hair on his body stood on end. He told Sue he wasn't sure what it was, but he knew something was in the room.

Since Sue left in 1992, she hasn't been back to the brewery much, though she's heard there haven't been many other sightings. She has no explanation but suggests, "Maybe we were just initially receptive enough that he felt comfortable appearing around us. Maybe people aren't as receptive now. I don't know. It's wacky."

7

Spirits of
Schools and Stages

South Eugene High School

Pat Avery, the drama instructor at South Eugene High
School, says that recently there hasn't been much activity
from the ghost that is now famous for haunting their auditorium. "Although it sometimes seems to be a noisy place with
random sounds," he admits, "everyone is aware that it might
be the spirit of a student who died falling from the catwalk."

Pat has been teaching at the school for only two years, but
he has heard all the stories and is familar with the ghost's history. In the late 1950s, a student named Robert Granke fell
from the upper story of the auditorium. He landed on the
audience seating and was killed. Since then, some people sitting in the seat where he died claim to feel a cold chill. There
is a melodramatic story about a brick falling from the ceiling
onto the seat just before a patron sat down. That one is particularly strange and disturbing because the auditorium is a
wooden structure.

In an article written for the Eugene *Register-Guard* in the
mid-1970s, Mike O'Brien wrote about several people who
had chilling firsthand tales of their run-ins with whatever it
is that calls the auditorium home. Former drama director
David Nale generally took a pragmatic approach to the
occurrences; however, there was one time when he thought
he saw something.

There's a huge space between the ceiling of the auditorium
and the attic. Tall enough to stand up in, it's a rabbit-warren
of narrow corridors, boxes and reinforcement structures.
Ladders nailed to the wall lead up to a trapdoor. Whenever
there was a strange noise, David Nale would have to investigate. On one of his trips through the dark, creepy tangle of
cables and pulleys, he thought he saw someone in a white

shirt. He followed the glow until he walked right into the wall. When the lights came on, he realized there wasn't a door nearby. Whatever it was had passed right through the wall.

Graduate Maxine Walton had experiences that led her to believe the spirit is not friendly. At first, she felt someone was watching her when she worked backstage. Then she noticed props were disappearing during rehearsals for a performance of *The Bad Seed*, a play about evil. But it was the incident during a run of *Man of La Mancha* that gave her chills. Up in the balcony in the walkway, Maxine saw a blue figure looking back at her. She ran to find the director, but there was nothing to see by the time they returned.

During a summer production of *West Side Story*, Vikki DeGaa got the distinct feeling she was not alone on stage. She and another woman arrived early to run light cues in advance of the evening's performance. After the auditorium was darkened, the lights were brought up individually. Vikki stood on stage while the other woman tested the lights one by one. As she stood there in the dark, Vikki suddenly heard the distinct sound of someone walking upstairs. The sound came from the ceiling at the back of the auditorium. While she listened, the footsteps moved slowly and deliberately in her direction.

With the footsteps finally overhead, Vikki forced herself to look up into the open spaces in the ceiling. She saw a flash of light—something that looked like legs passing in front of the opening. Then whatever it was disappeared. The women confirmed they both heard the spooky sound.

Other people working late at night have looked up into the balcony and seen a bluish figure. By the time they go to investigate, the elusive shape is gone. Another former student walked on stage and flicked on the lights, surprising someone up in the balcony. But the room had been locked and there was no way in without a key. No one was there when he went to see who had sneaked in.

While cleaning in the theater, custodians have also reported looking up into the balcony and seeing a young man sitting there. They call him down and go to check it out, but no one is ever there. The balcony is now closed off—it was causing acoustic problems for the performances—but strange noises still emanate from it.

Jefferson Davis' book, *Ghosts and Strange Critters of Washington and Oregon,* includes a story that may suggest the ghost is not a malevolent spirit. In 1994, a worker who was sweeping the roof above the auditorium suddenly fell through a weak spot. He dropped 35 feet onto the seats of the theater below. Rescue workers were shocked to find the man bruised and shaken but very much alive. His only injury was a broken foot. Did a supernatural hand guide the falling man to a soft landing? Regardless of the answer to that question, his survival is almost as bizarre as the other events that take place in South Eugene High School's auditorium.

George Harding's Ghost

People who like to add a little extra thrill to their theater-going experiences might wish to visit the city of Monmouth in the Willamette Valley. It is home to the beautiful Western Oregon University campus and its spacious fine arts theater, the Rice Auditorium. Locals say the ghost of former drama teacher George Harding still lurks backstage. Lights turn on or off, sets topple over and mysterious footsteps have been heard on stage when the theater is supposed to be empty.

The current head of the WOU theater and dance department, Dr. Richard Davis, knew George Harding. He met the dedicated teacher in 1964 when he joined the university faculty. Dr. Davis remembers Harding as an interesting man, "very gruff" and completely involved in his work. Harding carried a heavy course load, teaching both speech and theater. He also directed plays and was involved in the Salem Community Theatre. In addition to being a talented teacher, Harding was an excellent thespian.

When Harding arrived in Monmouth in 1946, the dramatic arts were suffering. He worked tirelessly to resurrect a regular theatrical season with a series of plays. Harding also got permission to establish a chapter of the national theater fraternity, Alpha Psi Omega, in Monmouth. With the aim of encouraging dramatic production at every step in a student's academic career, Alpha Psi Omega has sponsored the formation of theater honor societies in high schools and junior colleges throughout the United States since 1921.

In October 1962, a colossal Columbus Day storm destroyed the auditorium in what was then the Oregon College of Education. The theater department temporarily moved into the old Monmouth High School gymnasium while awaiting the construction of a new facility on the WOU campus. Drama professor George Harding , however, wouldn't have a chance to move into the Rice Auditorium, because he suddenly became ill and died of a heart attack in 1965, well before its completion.

But Harding had been planning for the new building, saving up props and, more significantly, lights that would be used in the new theater. Richard Davis says Harding was so concerned that the new building be properly equipped that he had been hoarding lights to install there.

The strange incidents began soon after Harding's death in the summer of 1965. Technical director Dean Borland noticed an odd pattern of behavior with the lights in the old high school. He would turn them out at one end of the building, but by the time he walked through to the other end, the lights would turn back on. Richard Davis says he experienced the phenomenon himself and knows it to be true. He recalls, "I can remember turning lights out and having them come back on again, and there's a kind of strangeness to that." Professor Davis says other people who worked in the old building late at night told him they also experienced weird, eerie things with the lights.

The new Rice Auditorium building finally opened in 1976. Soon after moving in, some members of the theater arts program got some disconcerting signs that perhaps George had figured out where they were now located.

Before his death, Allen Adams, former associate professor of theater arts and a theater designer at WOU, related some strange occurrences in the first week of the theater's operation. A group of people in the basement were startled by a hard thump and a swoosh sound from the floor above them.

The spirit of former drama instructor George Harding lurks backstage at Western Oregon University's Rice Auditorium.

Everyone ran upstairs and found the fire curtain had fallen to the stage. The curtain had been held up by heavy lead links designed to melt in a fire, but there was no fire.

The logical explanation for the falling curtain, according to Adams, would be that the summer heat had produced temperatures up in the fly loft area that were high enough to melt the links. It was common for the temperature to hit 120° F during the height of summer. But Adams was more inclined to believe that George Harding was behind the incident. Adams told a reporter for the *Sunday Oregonian*, "I guess old George found out where we were." Adams' theory was that by dropping the curtain, George was letting everyone know he was still around.

Other people have heard things that make them wonder if Adams is right. Performers in the women's dressing room, which is located right under the stage, have heard someone walking on the boards above. But when they went to see who was up there, the theater was empty. Could George have been doing one last technical check before show time?

More intriguing are the ongoing issues with the lights. After moving into the Rice Auditorium, Dean Borland also observed strange things happening, such as the lights turning on and off by themselves, as they had in the school theater. In the mid-1990s, bizarre events occurred when Borland was in the building late in the evening, hanging lights or fixing things for the set. He told Richard Davis the lights would go out when there was no reason for them to malfunction. Davis says he understands Borland's concern. "In the old building you could say it was just the old wiring, but you wouldn't think that would be a problem in the new facility," he explains. The thought was that George Harding was still watching out for "his" lights.

Adding to the strangeness was the presence of a mysterious white cat. Davis tells me there used to be sightings of the white cat around the old high school building, and once in a while he is spotted in the new building. "It seemed odd," says Davis, "That it would come around, then disappear."

George Harding continues to maintain a presence in the theater that he loved so dearly. The students thought he should receive some sort of tribute, so they put on shows to finance the purchase and framing of his portrait. The picture of Professor Harding still hangs in an alcove area adjacent to the lobby.

Southern Oregon University

Southern Oregon University was called the Southern Oregon Normal School when its first building (Churchill Hall) was dedicated in 1926. It became a women's school during the 1930s and '40s. After the Second World War, the campus expanded. Now the university offers liberal arts and science courses to over 5500 students. And, like many college campuses, the students have some pretty amazing tales of ghostly encounters. There's the ghoulish janitor with the wandering hands in the Britt Hall. Or there's the ghostly security guard in Taylor Hall on permanent posthumous patrol.

Churchill Hall

The second floor of this gorgeous building is the one with the ghosts. Churchill Hall is the oldest building on campus, a stately brick structure with ivy-covered walls and a sense of timeless elegance. It houses the university's administrative offices on the first floor. Upstairs there is a lecture hall, offices and an auditorium with a large stage. Whatever spirit lives there has a sense of humor and likes to play around with the lights in the projection booth.

In the late 1980s, a group of students were practicing for a speech class presentation. As evening approached, the room became dark, so one of the students called for someone to turn on the lights. The lights came on almost instantly, allowing the group to continue working on their project. Several minutes passed before anyone realized that no one from the group had left to turn on the lights. Then someone realized that the projection booth, where the lights are operated, was locked. There would have been no way to get in. The students ran from the auditorium without looking back.

In another instance involving the projection booth, a student reported seeing someone in the booth. The apparition didn't move but generated a menacing presence. A security guard was summoned, but when he shone a light into the booth there was nothing there. Nevertheless, the feeling persisted and the guard didn't waste any time getting out of the room.

The phantom also sets high standards for student behavior while in the auditorium. Foul language is simply not tolerated. Some students have reported feeling their hair tugged or their cheeks slapped if they uttered a profanity. Others have noticed a sudden burning sensation in their mouths.

Although most of the experiences have been fairly tame, there was a report from one student who insisted that he heard gobbling sounds while he was cleaning the auditorium floor. The horrible noise came from behind a curtain on the stage, and was accompanied by the stench of rotting meat. The student didn't stick around to find out what might be lurking behind the curtain.

Taylor Hall

It takes true dedication to show up for work after you're dead. Perhaps the spirit of a security guard still on patrol at Taylor Hall may not realize he is part of a different kind of alumni—the cadre of dearly departed.

The phantom security guard is apparently the ghost of a former student who graduated from the college in the late 1960s with a degree in criminology. He worked at the college for the next 20 years as a security guard. Focusing on Central and Taylor Halls, he made sure that he was scheduled on those routes as often as possible. Not coincidentally, Taylor Hall was the home of the criminology department.

One day in the late 1980s, the guard left early complaining of chest pains. He went to have them checked out. A woman who worked in Taylor Hall and was close friend of his saw him later that same day. Still in uniform, he stopped by her office to tell her that he had to run out but would return soon. She assumed he still hadn't gone to check out those chest pains. Imagine her surprise when someone called just moments after seeing the guard to tell her that he had died of a massive heart attack. His death occurred at about the time when she had seen him.

Since the guard's death, he has been seen by staff and students on several occasions. One faculty member had an encounter that prompted her to take better care of her keys. She had a habit of leaving her office and returning at night to find the door locked. Usually not a problem, on one night it happened that she left her purse inside and could not get into the office. It was after 10 PM and Taylor Hall was empty, so the only hope of getting into the office was to leave and call security. Just as she was about to search for a phone, she heard a man's voice behind her. An older security guard in a blue uniform asked if she needed to get into her office. When she replied that her purse was locked inside, he obligingly unlocked the door. She gratefully went in to retrieve her bag, and then stepped out to thank him for being helpful, but he was gone. It seemed odd but she didn't think too much of it. Not until later that night. At home, the professor suddenly realized that the university security guards wore gray or brown uniforms. They hadn't used blue uniforms in a decade.

An anthropology student named Jon had two run-ins with the guard's ghost. On the first occasion, he had been poking about in Taylor Hall's storage spaces, exploring the various things left behind over the years. He found a photograph of a security guard posing out in front Taylor Hall. In the picture, the guard was proudly holding his college diploma. While Jon stood there examining the picture, he realized he wasn't alone. Turning around, he saw the same security guard—only older—and not very pleased. The guard took the photograph and told Jon not to poke around in the storage rooms without help. The guard warned that the boxes were precariously stacked and might crash down on him if he wasn't careful. With that, the guard left. Later, the student told others who had seen the ghost guard and they confirmed his description.

The second encounter was less pleasant. Jon was cleaning up after a late night session with the Anthropology Club. It was after 11 PM, but the group's boxes had to be put back in the storage room near the basement boiler room. Jon was tired and wanted to go home, but went downstairs only to find the room locked. He was looking for a janitor when he noticed the door to the boiler room was slightly open. This was unusual, as the door was normally bolted shut. He could also see light inside and some movement. Although he was getting very creepy feelings, Jon thought the person in the room was a janitor who could help him unlock his storage unit, so he could put everything away and go home.

He approached the boiler room door and froze ten feet in front it. The security guard he had seen before—the one who everyone said was a ghost—stepped out in front of him and ordered him to put the stuff in his car and get out. Immediately. Then the guard went back into the boiler room and closed the door. From under the door, Jon could see the light go out. He grabbed the box, ran to his car and raced home.

Britt Hall

Jon might have had better luck finding a janitor over at Britt Hall, but the experience would not have been any more pleasant.

Britt Hall is the second oldest building on campus. Originally called Memorial Court, it housed the gymnasium and physical education facilities when it opened in 1936. After a new gymnasium was built in the 1950s, Memorial Court was converted into a student union building and renamed in memory of Amalia Britt and her brother, Emil, the last of pioneer photographer Peter Britt's family.

As in Churchill Hall, the ghost seems to prefer the second floor. The stories suggest that the spirit of a janitor who used to work in the building in the 1950s is responsible for the odd things that happen there. The man wasn't all that pleasant while alive—he was a chain-smoker with a raspy voice and roving hands that didn't discriminate between female and male students.

Students have reported being followed by someone with a raspy cough and labored breathing, but no one is visible when they turn to look. Others say an old man followed them and tried to reach out and touch them.

Britt Hall now houses the registrar's office, the university's admissions office and the communications department. Kim Olson, the communications office manager, says she hasn't seen the creepy janitor but has become well acquainted with a soldier ghost who regularly walks down the hall past her office. Apparently, Britt Hall was used briefly as a barracks, and the soldier may still be following orders on a path to nowhere.

The ghost is quite clear from the waist up "though translucent," and he is three dimensional. Although his footsteps attract Kim's attention, he has no visible legs. "He looks like he's in his thirties. He's wearing a brownish-green jacket, military cut, and he has a hat or cap." The first time Kim saw him walk past, she was working late and everyone else had gone home. "I knew I was the only one in the building. I called out, 'There's nobody down there,' but he kept walking toward the department chair's office. I didn't hear any door open or close, so I went out to look and he had disappeared." Kim hunted around, but there was no sign of the officer. He didn't go past her. It was winter and getting dark, so Kim quickly packed up and left.

Since then, she says the ghost has become a familiar presence, showing up two or three times a term. The legless apparition always walks in the same direction, though not always at night, and never turns to look when Kim calls out a greeting. "Now I'm used to him," she told me. "I usually see him out of my peripheral vision, and by the time I turn around I just see his back walking down the hall. I'll call out a hello but he never responds."

Other people working in Britt Hall have also encountered ghosts, though they may not be the same one that Kim sees. A new faculty member came to Kim's office one day asking if there were ghosts in the building. She had heard doors opening and closing when no one was nearby. Kim says she has also encountered doors that open and shut by themselves. "I smell things all the time too. Roses or oranges. Sometimes I can clearly smell tobacco. Every time all the hairs on my body stand up." Maybe she has encountered the chain-smoking custodian after all.

Mount Angel College

A former student of Mount Angel College relayed this ghost story about a female spirit in the school theater. The college was originally established in 1887 as part of the Mount Angel Abbey. It continued the work of Benedictine monk Father Adelhelm Odermatt, the abbey's founder.

Father Adelhelm was charged with the task of founding a monastery that would serve as a place of refuge, should the abbey in his Swiss homeland be suppressed. He explored Nebraska, Colorado, California and Washington before settling in 1882 in a rural area of western Oregon in the Willamette Valley. Father Adelhelm named the site Mount Angel. The monks bought up various tracts of land on a hilltop and began building the monastery and seminary. The newly appointed Archbishop Gross, Oregon City's third archbishop, arrived at Mount Angel in 1885. As an educator, he insisted the community open a college, so Mount Angel College was built two years later.

The monks were assisted in their work by the Benedictine Sisters of Queen of Angels Monastery. At the request of Father Adelhelm, six sisters and four novices made their way from a Benedictine convent in the Swiss Alps to the hilltop in Mount Angel. The sisters taught at a second Mount Angel College established as a "women only" school at the south end of the town.

Initially, Mount Angel College was an extension of the local high school. Sister Alberta Deeker is the Benedictine Sisters' historian. She says the school on their campus began as a normal school for women that offered an extra two years of courses. It eventually became a teacher's college. In 1954, the college expanded to include men. The college then received accreditation to offer a four-year liberal arts program, which was particularly strong in art and drama. It was in the drama department that all the extra ghostly activity supposedly took place.

A graduate of the college's gerontology program told me that she heard there was a ghost in the auditorium where the drama students practiced and performed. The woman, who requested anonymity, said that every time the students performed a play, a woman who had worked in the drama department before her death would show up to watch the performance from the upper projection booth where the stage lights were situated. Many students would look up to see the woman's apparition gazing at the stage.

Sister Alberta laughed at this story, but confirmed that rumors of a ghost persisted at the college. "It was a great thing among the students. Many of them said that it was the ghost of Sister Beatrice. Whether it was a fantasy or not, I don't know. I never saw any ghost. But it was definitely a story that the students loved to keep alive." Sister Beatrice taught drama before her death, and Sister Alberta said she was a German woman with a very forceful personality. Could it be that she still wanted to direct the acting students from beyond the grave?

The sister was buried in the graveyard two or three blocks from the drama department's auditorium. But for some unknown reason, the woman's grave site would always sink. Every year, groundskeepers would take off the sod and add dirt, but the grave sank anyway.

Mount Angel College closed in 1973 when it became no longer financially viable to run the small school. At its peak, about 400 students were enrolled.

The Bagdad Theater

It was built in 1927, during Hollywood's infancy, to be an "oasis of entertainment." Universal Pictures sank a whopping $100,000 into the celluloid palace. Its decor capitalized on the popularity of silent movies like *The Thief of Bagdad* with Middle-Eastern decorations, a gurgling fountain and usherettes in Arabian-style uniforms. It was also used for live vaudeville shows, and boasted of a personal appearance by Hollywood's Marilyn Mills "with her famous horse, Beverly" as a theater highlight.

Who knew Portland's Bagdad Theater would also end up as a wellspring for ghost hunters? It's hardly surprising. Manager Jason McEllrath says it is a big, old and very creepy building, especially after dark. The Hawthorne Boulevard theater has seen it all. As the Bagdad rounds out a century of cinematic enchantment, the stories of a presence that looms off-screen continue to enthrall lovers of the paranormal.

It's been quiet at the Bagdad for a while now. Jason says the inexplicable events don't recur that often. But he does admit that employees have told him of garbage cans that roll by themselves through the kitchen. Jason believes that wheels and a sloped floor are the source of that story; others, however, link it to the legend of the unhappy janitor.

Perhaps the pervasive frivolity was too much for the janitor. Or maybe the constant buzz of theater people finally got to him. But one night, after the performances ended, he hanged himself backstage. His body was found the following day. Nowadays, employees working backstage occasionally feel they are being watched. Others have reported feeling a sudden cold chill. Maybe it's just the pesky noose that still hangs from the rafters that is stoking over-active

A janitor ghost is said to haunt the historic Bagdad Theater in Portland

imaginations. Or maybe the janitor was such a perfectionist about how things should be cleaned that he couldn't rest knowing others might not do as good a job as he did. You know what they say—if you want something done well, do it yourself. By the sounds of it, the ghostly janitor took those words not only to heart, but to his grave and back again among the living.

Vera, the Ghost of Knight Hall

At Forest Grove's Pacific University, popular campus myth has it that at least one ghostly spirit (and possibly as many as two or three) inhabits Knight Hall. The legend—not to mention many a visitor—suggests that a female spirit named Vera watches over the stately Victorian house.

Knight Hall was constructed in 1897 as President Sidney Harper Marsh's second home. It is named after Frank L. Knight, a trustee and benefactor of the university. Knight Hall was remodeled in 1946 and turned into a coed dormitory. In 1953, it became Phi Beta Tau's fraternity house. By the 1970s, it had become the music building. That's when some of the first stories of a spectral presence emerged.

According to a 1971 account in Margaret Read MacDonald's *Ghost Stories From the Pacific Northwest*, a student encountered a very vocal spirit as he was making his rounds as night watchman. Shortly before he locked up the hall, he heard a woman singing in the third floor library. Surprised at the late night practice session, he climbed the stairs to tell the singer it was time to leave. But when he reached the third floor, the singing abruptly stopped. The watchman opened the library door to find it empty. He hunted for a practical joker, but found no one. When he searched for a hidden tape recorder, he again discovered nothing.

Deciding to check out the rest of building in case someone had slipped by him, the watchman searched the second floor and was on his way to the first level when he saw her. Floating in front of him was a bluish white apparition of a woman. She drifted in front of a professor's office, then disappeared.

A few years later, in 1979, two reporters from the student paper spent the night in an attempt to flush out the ghost. It didn't take long. During the night, they heard footsteps, lights went out, an alto voice sang and long skirts rustled by. When one of the reporters played the piano—apparently quite badly—a woman's voice whispered emphatically in his ear, "Please stop!"

Admissions counselor Jeff Grundon knows the stories are true. His encounters with Vera number in the dozens. Prior to Vera, Jeff says he was a "total skeptic." He vividly recalls his first meeting with her. He was moving into his new office on a hot July evening several years ago. Despite the late hour, the temperature was still in the high 80s, and Jeff had opened a window to create a breeze. As he assembled his desk, Jeff suddenly felt a cold chill that gave him goosebumps and set all the hair on his neck on end. He had the distinct feeling someone was watching him, but there was no one to be seen.

Later that same evening, he went down the hall to check his mail. The pigeonholes were by the old back stairwell. Jeff had his back to the door, which was propped open with a wooden floor stopper. He heard the stopper being dragged along the floor and realized that somehow the door had shut. But when he went to pull it open, the door wouldn't release. He had to yank it a few times before it opened. Then he noticed the bell on the handle. It usually rang every time he moved the door—but it hadn't made a sound when the door closed. Since then, the ghost has locked bathroom doors, tossed bins off storage room shelves, turned lights on and off and walked tirelessly up and down the stairs at night.

"One of the more interesting encounters I had was on the third floor with support staff members and a work study student," recalls Jeff. "There was a box fan on the floor. We were talking about new projects and the fan turned on by itself full blast."

In the summer of 1997, assistant basketball coach Jason Morgenthaler was an undergrad working in the admissions office. Intrigued by all the stories, Jason and one of his friends brought a Ouija board and a group of witnesses to the third floor and spent the night talking to the ghost. During the first conversation, they asked her test questions to prove that she, and not they, were moving the pointer. Her correct answers sent half the witnesses scurrying out in fear. "It was pretty intense," says Jason. "I could feel her moving my hand." Pressing on, they determined her name was Vera. Jason says they believe she died in the building as a young girl, and that her father was a music professor. They returned for a second night of questioning, and Vera responded. She apparently indicated that other spirits live in the house as well, and that she oversees them. She refused, however, to say how she died, leaving unresolved the rumors that she was murdered.

For alumni and professors alike, there's no question that Vera is a permanent resident of Knight Hall.

Will Charles Laughton
Please Take a Bow?

Theaters provide perfect homes for ghosts. The stage alone is evocative of any number of imagined realities. Many theaters hold the spirits of hundreds of actors, some of whom may still be trying to tread the boards for one more ovation.

Several stories of ghosts haunt the theatres at Ashland's Shakespeare Festival. The festival in the southern Oregon city has blossomed into an eight-month event running from April to November. Three theaters perform both Shakespearean and contemporary productions. The best ghost stories originate in the Elizabethan Theatre, where Shakespeare's stories of love, tragedy and spiritual transformation are presented by starlight in the 1200-seat open-air theatre. It's also where the spirit of Charles Laughton is said to exist.

Beth Bardossi, the publications associate for the festival, was happy to relate the history of hauntings. In fact, she is in the process of writing her own book of ghost stories. Although Beth has worked for the Oregon Shakespeare Festival for 21 years, she says with some disappointment that she has never met anyone who actually bumped into Charles Laughton's spirit. There haven't been any reports of activity in quite a few years. But a number of facts may explain why Laughton hung around after his death.

It turns out that the film actor desperately wanted to play King Lear on stage. And he wanted to do it at the Elizabethan Theatre. Angus L. Bowmer, producing director of the festival, explains Laughton's connection to the festival in his book, *As I Remember, Adam: An Autobiography of a Festival*. The story is as sad as it is interesting. Charles Laughton initially snubbed Angus Bowmer, but after he saw a production in 1961 he changed his tune. Laughton stayed for four days, delaying a Hollywood movie, so that he could watch all the plays. Two weeks later, he telephoned Angus Bowmer and begged to play the part of Lear. In his book, Bowmer recalls the actor saying, "I am throwing myself at you. I want to play with that wonderful company of yours, and it won't cost you a cent."

It was agreed that Charles Laughton would come in 1963, after the filming of *Irma La Douce* in Paris. It was possible that he might also portray Falstaff in *The Merry Wives of Windsor*. Unfortunately, Laughton died in 1962 before he could act in the movie or return to Ashland. That summer, his disembodied spirit was heard laughing loudly backstage during performances of *The Merry Wives of Windsor*. He was also seen wearing the costume of Falstaff. And in the performance of *King Lear* that year, eerie noises heard by both cast and audience were attributed to Laughton. Since then, patrons and actors say they have heard sighs throughout the theatre. Most people identify them as those of Mr. Laughton.

Columbia Gorge
Community College

Of the original complex, eleven of the twelve buildings remain to comprise what is now Columbia Gorge Community College. In the 1920s, the complex was a hospital for tuberculosis patients. Then it became a minimum security facility for the mentally ill. In 1980, it became the Judson Baptist College. As of 1993, it has been home to the community college. It's also been home to a few stray ghosts.

There are reports of apparitions and strange occurrences in some of the older buildings on campus, such as the former nurses' residence (that now stands empty) and the Kevorkian Building before it was taken down in the late 1990s.

These days, the campus concentrates most activities in four of the buildings. The Skill Center, or Adult Learning Center, is the latest source of spooky stories. In 1996, the college hired painters to refresh the fourth-floor walls in the learning center. Their work did not agree with someone or something on the fourth floor. They couldn't put their paintbrushes down for a second or they would disappear. Lids on paint cans that had just been opened would be sealed shut if the painters turned their backs. One painter felt something hit him on the back while he was standing on a ladder. It wasn't enough to deter them from the work, but the painters were happy to finish the job.

When I called to confirm the stories, the contact person for the Skill Center said she had heard of the ghost stories, but didn't know of anything recent. She hasn't had any encounters herself in the building with mischievous spirits, but she also didn't seem to think that it was out of the realm of possibility. Richard, who works in the college library, has been at Columbia Gorge for a couple of years and he hadn't heard anything about phantoms on campus. Maybe now that the complex is a more serious center of learning, the prankster ghosts find it a lot less fun to hang around.

Swedenburg House

Could it be that certain fertile imaginations in a large student body have created the ghost stories about Swedenburg House? Or is it only natural that a massive old manor in the center of a university should be haunted? Either way, it doesn't take long for visitors to hear about the little pig-tailed girl who has been sighted on the property. Not to mention the night time visits by people who got through locked doors to leave imprints on the beds.

Sitting at the edge of Southern Oregon University, the mansion is distinguished by its colonnaded porch and an expansive second-floor balcony that wraps around two sides of the structure. Its ghosts have become the stuff of campus legend, although some skeptics say it is pure fiction.

The turn-of-the-century building is named after its first owner, Dr. F.G. Swedenburg. A prominent doctor who lived there from 1919 to 1937, he died suddenly while traveling in Europe. The university acquired the property in 1966. It ceased to be used for residences, and campus development and alumni offices moved into the second floor. The first floor holds displays for the Southern Oregon Historical Society. For a few years after it was purchased, the house sat empty. That's when the majority of the ghost stories started.

Bill Meulemans taught political science in the early 1970s when the house had just come into the university's possession. He didn't see anything himself, but he had an experience on the second floor that sent him scurrying. Bill had heard the rumors that security guards were reporting weird experiences such as finding kitchen cupboard doors open after they'd made sure everything was in order before locking up.

More intriguing were the tales of slept-in beds, despite the locked doors. Three separate security guards apparently found that upstairs beds—usually made up for display purposes—would have indentations each morning as if someone had been lying on them. They were sure the doors had been locked and that no one could get in the building. None of the guards realized that each was encountering the same phenomenon until some time later.

The coincidence encouraged Bill Meulemans to bring in some candles and a Ouija board one night for an experiment. He and three friends sat on the second floor and made contact with something that set them on edge.

Most experts in paranormal and ghost research will tell you that Ouija boards are a dangerous way to communicate with the spirit world. Although they are only pieces of pressed wood available at almost any toy or occult store, they can serve as uncontrolled portals to another plane, through which malevolent spirits can enter to our world.

One Internet website explains that spirits contacted through a Ouija reside on "the lower astral plane." These spirits are often very confused and may have died violent or sudden deaths. If they are contacted, they could become dangerous to those using the board. Another problem is that multiple spirits may attempt to come through at the same time. Apparently, the real danger lies in asking for physical proof of their existence. Asking a spirit to turn on a light or close a window "opens a doorway" and allows it to enter the physical world.

For Bill and his group, the Ouija board told them of a suicide attempt by one of the students in the room—a secret that none of them had known. Then the board jumped a few feet in the air. The terrified group immediately bolted down the stairs. The security officer who had accompanied them was the last out, and as he locked up he was unable to move his hand off the doorknob for several seconds, as if someone was holding it there.

Joey Ngan believes there's a ghost in the house. As director of campus security, he was skeptical at first. He'd heard people's claims about fleeting glimpses of a little girl in pinafore and pigtails. In fact, he was prompted by those stories to show respect by announcing his presence whenever he entered for an inspection of the premises.

In 1983, a state-of-the-art security system was installed as part of some restoration work on the house. During rounds one night, Joey and another guard checked in to make sure the house was empty and that the system was working. They locked up and left to continue checking the rest of the campus. Sometime later, they drove past Swedenburg House, and under the porch light on the first floor Joey saw a woman in a dress sitting by a window. His partner saw the same thing. They checked the house out but found it empty. The room where they'd seen the woman was still locked.

Even so, some local historians say there are no ghosts. One retired journalist came right out and called the claims a hoax. There haven't been many new stories in a while. For those who dare, it might be time for another Ouija board session.

8

Oregon City's
Haunted History

• • •

Maybe it's the scenic location, but a remarkable number of Oregon's haunted houses are in Oregon City. The following houses all have lengthy records of strange, inexplicable events. Some have ghosts, some don't. But for people seeking a one-on-one otherworldly experience, many of these homes have been turned into public museums where visitors just might encounter one of Oregon's founding fathers or some member of their family still in residence.

• • •

McLoughlin House

Dr. John McLoughlin, the state-legislated "Father of Oregon," died in the parlor of his Georgian-style mansion from diabetes complications in 1857. Could it be that the Canadian-born medic still inhabits the house, along with his Chippewa wife, Marguerite? The house is now a museum, and many visitors report seeing strange things, including the doctor's custom-built rocking chair moving by itself.

Originally from Quebec, Dr. McLoughlin was lured west by the fur trade. As a superintendent for the Hudson's Bay Company, he crossed the Rockies in 1824 and established Fort Vancouver on the Columbia River in 1825. Although he was a shrewd businessman, he had a generous streak—giving supplies to struggling pioneers—that eventually cost him his job. He built his mansion along the banks of the Willamette River and moved into it with his family in 1846 after being forced to retire. In 1909, the house was saved from demolition and moved to the hilltop area of Oregon City. It remained deathly quiet until the mid-1970s. But some of the house's creaks and groans are hard to explain. Doors slam shut. Objects fall to the floor. Footsteps can be heard. Some people firmly believe there is at least one ghost in McLoughlin House, possibly more. The entity is thought to be none other than the home's original master, who in life stood six foot four, astonishingly tall for the time.

Denise McGee, a former curator of McLoughlin House, downplays the ghost stories of chairs that mysteriously rock by themselves or tall shadows that duck to pass through the doorways. "Dr. McLoughlin has not introduced himself to me," she says with a laugh. Although good-humored about the tales, Denise said she had not experienced anything that could be attributed to an unearthly presence. She did have one odd experience around Halloween in the upstairs bedroom. Denise heard what sounded like a step. She heard it again, and thinking it might be rain leaking through the roof and hitting the floor, she investigated. There was nothing in the room. However, she noticed a footstool was shoved up against the foot rail of the bed. She says that when she pulled it away, "the bed skirt started dancing, moving all by itself." Unnerved by the experience, Denise went back the next day and repeated her actions—with the same results. On closer inspection, she discovered the bed skirt was attached by stretchy elastic. Her conclusion: "I think it's because people have heard the stories, so they're more susceptible to believing that what they see is the result of a ghost."

But Denise's predecessor had several encounters with her spectral "boss." Nancy Wilson was curator of the museum home for 20 years, during which time she met up with Dr. McLoughlin's ghost on more than one occasion. "I think there is a ghost in the McLoughlin House," she told a reporter for the *Oregonian* in 1987. Maybe more than one, she adds.

The spirit of John McLoughlin, the so-called "Father of Oregon,"
maintains an imposing presence at his former home in Oregon City.

"One five-year-old boy came up to me during one of our
summer tours and told me, 'I know there are ghosts in here,' "
she recalls. Another tourist told her she had seen Dr.
McLoughlin's rocking chair rocking back and forth in an
empty room upstairs.

Nancy would occasionally hear the thud of boots walking
along the upstairs hallways. On one occasion, she felt a tap
on her shoulder, but when she turned around there was
no one nearby. On more than one occasion, she saw a tall
shadow ducking through doorways. Nancy Wilson was sure
it was the doctor. "I think it's the ghost of McLoughlin. He
was a tall man."

The incident that convinced her she wasn't hallucinating—
or that the events weren't a product of her imagination—
took place in the dining room. Nancy and a co-worker

witnessed two of five glass prisms on a candlestick move as if someone were flicking them. The other three remained motionless. The former curator believes they couldn't have moved by themselves.

Denise McGee told me of one woman touring through the downstairs rooms who said she felt someone's hands on her shoulder, pushing her until she almost fell over. There are also accounts from visitors who claim to have seen a woman in the upstairs window. Perhaps McLoughlin's wife stayed behind to keep him company.

Then there is the ghost of a little black-and-white dog that runs through the house. Visitors have inquired about the little dog they have seen walking through the hall. Former curator Nancy Wilson insists that no such dog existed while she worked there. However, on two separate occasions Wilson swears she saw tiny paw prints on one of the rugs in a small room on the first floor that is off limits to visitors and well isolated from the rest of the house. Her opinion is that it is unlikely a dog could have sneaked into the house during a tour, because it would have left the same prints through the rest of the house.

In the parlor—the same room in which McLoughlin died—hangs a portrait of the doctor. Each September 3, on the anniversary of his death, the portrait is apparently lit by an oval of sunlight at 9:35 AM. Although the date of McLoughlin's death is known, the exact hour of his death cannot be verified.

But why would McLoughlin haunt his own house? After two decades as curator in the house, Nancy Wilson developed several theories for the doctor's restless spirit. "Maybe it's because he was mad at people who didn't accept his family [because his wife was part Chippewa]," Wilson speculates. Or it might be linked to all the activity in the house after his death. After Dr. McLoughlin's wife died, the house went through many incarnations—from hotel to brothel to boarding house.

The physician's spirit may also have been uprooted—literally—when his gravesite was moved. For 91 years, his bones rested peacefully in the graveyard of a Roman Catholic church. In 1948, the church property was sold, and both the doctor and his wife were dug up and moved to the corner of Fifth and Washington Streets, where the senior citizens' center is located. But they would not find everlasting rest there, either. In 1970, they were moved agains to their current spot next to the old house.

Although Denise McGee never got to meet the phantom doctor or his wife during her year at the house, she says she would have liked to make their acquaintance. She also wants to hear more compelling stories with details that can be corroborated, such as the style of dress worn by the ghosts.

Barclay House

Next to McLoughlin House is another historic site with a disembodied spirit, one who runs rather than walks. The former home of Dr. Forbes Barclay, the house is now maintained by the same historical society that oversees the McLoughlin property. The offices and gift shop for both sites reside in Barclay House.

After attempting to find the "northwest passage" in a reportedly disastrous voyage to the Arctic, Forbes Barclay came to the Pacific Northwest, just as his friend John McLoughlin did, as a physician for the Hudson's Bay Company. In the *Dictionary of Oregon History*, Dr. Forbes Barclay is described as an "Arctic explorer, physician, public official, philanthropist." Barclay built his house in 1849, and he and his wife, Maria Pambrum Barclay, and their seven children were prominent members of the Oregon City community. Dr. Barclay held several posts, including mayor, school superintendent and city coroner. The house stayed in the Barclay family until the 1930s, when it was moved in order to preserve it. The former apothecary is now an office. The formal parlor serves as a gift shop. The dining room and everyday parlor are meeting rooms that are open to the public. Although the function of the house has changed, could it be that some of the original residents have yet to find a new home?

For years, people have reported seeing a little red-haired boy playing in and around the house. The lad was first seen running around the house when the building was being used as the office of the Oregon City Chamber of Commerce. More than one person reported such a sighting, but no flesh-and-blood, red-haired boy was ever found.

Nancy Wilson, curator of the museum next door for two decades, told a reporter for the *Oregonian* that many years ago a woman who knew the previous owners of the house told her that a little boy had died in Barclay House. The death had occurred when the house was located on Main Street between Seventh and Eighth Streets in downtown Oregon City. Although there are no other details to confirm the boy's identity, the child is thought to be Forbes Barclay's young son. Alternatively, it may well have been one of Barclay's later descendents. The tombstone from the boy's grave disappeared some time ago, leaving his age and year of death a mystery. Barclay's Scottish roots could explain the shock of red hair, though.

In her book *Ghosts Stories of the Pacific Northwest*, Margaret Read MacDonald cites an intriguing example of paranormal activity in the house. In 1989, a five-year-old boy visiting the house with his parents asked the tour guide if the other little boy was supposed to be alone downstairs. Upon checking, the tour guide couldn't find another child. When he questioned the boy about the color of the other boy's hair, he was told it was red.

A municipal elevator was installed nearby because it is a steep walk up the hill from the river. A few years ago, elevator operator Sandy Tunison saw a boy outside the elevator door. He wore dark pants, boots and a wool jacket. She said his hair was clearly parted on the left and he was tall enough to put his chin on an ashtray mounted outside the elevator door. She looked away briefly to get her keys from the elevator panel, but he had vanished by the time she turned back.

But Denise McGee says the red-haired boy has not made an appearance recently.

With so many children in the Barclay family—seven in all—and mortality rates what they were 150 years ago, it is quite likely that more than one child may have died in the home. Whether or not the red-headed spirit continues to play in the hallways is subject to ongoing speculation.

Captain Phillips Bungalow

It's not enough that two houses on the same street are known to be haunted—apparitions have also been seen, felt or heard throughout most of the vast rooms in the nearby manor known as Captain Phillips Bungalow. The captain's magnificent mansion sits right across the street from Barclay House.

In the early 1900s, Phillips died of a heart attack while stoking the furnace in the basement. Recent owners say his spirit has set their hearts pounding several times. Sharyn Young told a reporter at the *Oregonian* in 1996 that since her family moved into the house in 1977, there had been too many poltergeist events to count. This is not just a case of sensing a presence. Bottles fly across rooms, utensils move off plates. During a party, a picture was sent flying to the floor.

Young would return home to find someone had redecorated. Picture frames on the walls would be empty. Each picture lay on the floor below—not tossed there, but carefully placed under the appropriate frame. Family portraits on the mantel were face down.

The events didn't bother Sharyn until it became clear her year-old granddaughter was being affected. The baby would wake up screaming, terrified of something. When Sharyn found the legs broken off a crystal figure hanging in the room, she decided it was time to act. She told the captain to stop because it was a baby's room. The direct approach had the desired effect. The haunting stopped—in that room at least.

In 1998, an accounting firm bought the house and initiated a major renovation. Carpets were torn up and the hardwood floors were restored. Walls and rooms were returned to their former condition. During the process, at least one odd thing happened to the contractor. He left the toilet paper in the bathroom, but when he returned the next day, it was sitting on the mantel—and he was the last person to lock up the house. Since then, however, there have been no incidents. Whenever there's a computer glitch, the accounting firm office workers will joke that Captain Phillips is around.

Amy, the office manager, told me she believes in ghosts. In her opinion, all is quiet because the renovations reflect the captain's original plan for the house. A relative of the previous owners once stopped by to see the new interior. He recounted an incident in which his family was sitting in the living room and they heard a crystal ashtray slide the whole length of the kitchen counter, then smash on the floor, although no one was in the kitchen at the time. Amy believes the new owners finally appeased the captain's sense of decor, so he is now content to leave the current residents alone.

Ermatinger House

Several ghosts live in Oregon City's oldest house. Just ask Marg and Rolla Harding, the property managers hired by the city to look after the house. Neither uses the word "haunted," though. "To me the term has a negative connotation," says Marg. "We've had nothing but positive experiences." And they've had lots of them.

Although the ghosts are not seen, their effects are plainly visible. Ribbons move from place to place, chairs slide away from tables and candlelight glides from room to room even when the house is empty. Passersby have reported seeing a woman in white carrying a lantern past an upstairs window.

Marg believes the events are closely tied to the house's past. Francis Ermatinger was another of the Hudson's Bay Company employees. Born in Portugal and educated in England, Ermatinger came to Oregon in 1825. He worked his way through the ranks under Dr. John McLoughlin, and was eventually appointed to run the company store in 1844. He also married McLoughlin's granddaughter, so the doctor told him to select a piece of property on which to live. The following year, Ermatinger built his home, the first frame house in Oregon City. It also had the unusual distinction of being the only square two-story Federal-style building with a flat roof. In 1910, the home was among those saved from encroaching development; it was moved to the town's upper level, just down the street from the McLoughlin and Barclay Houses.

During Ermatinger's residence, which was relatively short, the home was a social mecca for newcomers to the west. Ermatinger was a jovial, well-liked man who loved to entertain. It was at one of his parties when a coin toss determined the city of Portland's name. This may seem like a digression, but the story of the coin toss is oddly connected to the strange goings-on in the house.

In 1843, while canoeing on the Willamette, Asa Lovejoy and William Overton stopped to rest at a place referred to as the "clearing." The spot had good potential for a townsite, and the two men filed a claim. Soon afterward, Overton sold his half to Francis W. Pettygrove. Two years later, the "clearing" was named in an unusual way. Pettygrove, a merchant and a native of Maine, wanted to name the site "Portland," after his state's largest city. Lovejoy, a lawyer and a native of Massachusetts, favored calling it "Boston." At the time the two men were socializing at Ermatinger House, and to make the decision, they flipped a copper penny. Pettygrove won, and the "clearing" became Portland. The Pettygrove family donated the original "Portland Penny" to the Oregon History Center so that it could serve as a lasting reminder of the city's origins. It generally sits in a glass case in Ermatinger House.

Many families lived in the home after Ermatinger moved to Canada in 1848. More than a century passed, and in 1987 Ruth McBride Powers restored the house and ran it as a private museum until her death in 1993. McBride Powers' family continued to operate the museum for a while, but eventually asked the city to take over the deed. The house sat closed during the winter of 1996. That's where Marg and Rolla Harding come in.

Marg was asked by the city to operate the house and hold some teas for six months. After doing some research, she decided to hold living history teas set in 1865, at the end of the Civil War when the house had been transformed into a rooming house. For the teas, she dressed in period dress and gave her talks in the first person as if she was really living in the past.

Marg started hosting the teas three times a week in the spring of 1997. At first, there were no signs of spirits in the house, but it didn't take long for her to notice unusual occurrences. One day, the table was set for tea but no visitors came to the house. Marg left to go home, and her assistant Rocky closed up the house. He walked through the hall, past the dining room, to lock up the front door. When he went to walk back, a dining room chair that had been at the table was now blocking his path. It scared Rocky so much that he shared the experience with Marg. After hearing the story, Marg told me that she realized she had pushed the chair in several times the previous day, even though no one was there to move it. All day long she reset the chair, only to find it cocked out at an angle when she returned. The chair continued to move, so Marg playfully dubbed her spirit "The Captain." "I still didn't believe there was a ghost," says Marg.

At the same time, they discovered what appeared to be the spirit of a young girl in an upstairs bedroom. A china doll placed in a chair would move to the bed. Silk ribbons on the door handle unraveled by themselves, and clumps of the same colored silk thread would be found on the dresser. Marg named this phantom "April."

In 1999, a psychic medium came to the house when the Hardings were out. Without any previous knowledge of the events, the medium apparently told Rocky he felt a strong presence in the dining room. He said he knew that a well-dressed gentleman and former steamboat captain had taken up residence. The medium claimed that "Captain Williams" didn't die there, but had loved all the social activity that went on. Although the captain was confined to the dining room, the medium also picked up on the energy of a young

Several ghosts of the past haunt the eerily nondescript Ermatinger House.

girl who had died in the home. He said the girl, named April Spring, suffered from a long illness; her favorite things were her doll and silk ribbons. Marg has not been able to confirm the accuracy of his claims, but the coincidence with the names that she and the medium used nonetheless unnerved her.

In the following years, Marg and her husband Rolla experienced doors banging open or suddenly refusing to open. On a beautiful October day during a spirits of Halloween tea, Marg says one of their spirits got very playful. They couldn't keep the front door closed. It repeatedly flung open, despite being properly latched. But at the end of the day, as the last group was leaving, they couldn't get it open. No one could get out the front door. Rolla went out the back and around the house, to try to pull the door open, but it refused to budge. The group left by the rear entrance. As the house cleared, the front door suddenly opened again. They've also heard their names called when no one else was there. In spring 2000, Rolla was hanging drapery rods downstairs while Marg was working in a room upstairs. She heard him call her, so she yelled down to ask him what he wanted. Her husband said he hadn't said anything to her. "There was no doubt about it," she says. "I heard it over my right shoulder, in Rolla's voice." On a different occasion, Rolla also heard a soft voice call his name. He turned to answer, and realized no one was there.

For Marg, her most compelling story concerns the coin toss. In May 2001, school groups were touring through the historic houses in the area. Marg took her group into the parlor and told them about the coin toss, demonstrating with the actual 1838 penny. Those students moved on, and on her way to greet the next group Marg set the coin down on a table in the library. When she returned for it, the coin was gone. Panicked, she and all the teachers searched high and low. No coin. Heartsick, Marg thoroughly cleaned the house but never found the quarter-sized relic.

Nearly two months later, they prepared for fourth of July celebrations. Heavy rains had been leaking through the roof, and she and Rolla stopped by the house to check for damage. They found the house flooded, and in the rush to save rugs and furniture from more damage, Marg says she dumped her purse on the floor in the dining room. Once the mess was cleaned up, she retrieved her bag and went off to buy groceries. When she pulled her check book from a zippered pocket in her bag, out fell the old penny!

"I screamed," recalls an emotional Marg. "I started crying and the grocery clerk thought I had lost it." Marg figures the captain took the coin to keep it safe from the children that day and returned it to her at the first opportunity. She returned the coin to its display case in the house. "I feel like I'm trusted now," says Marg. "I still don't know what to make of these events and I don't know if they are ghosts, but my husband and I feel we're caretakers and that the care of the house has been entrusted to us, by both the city and whatever spirits live there."

Chairs still move. Ribbons unravel. Clumps of silk thread appear. And if you're lucky, you might hear your name whispered by one of the roving ghostly residents while enjoying an afternoon cup of tea.

The Camellia House

Bette Hayes is a straightforward, chatty woman in her mid-70s. But an experience in her former Victorian home left her at a loss for words. "It is a very vivid memory, even now," she says. Her husband, Karl, also had an experience that convinced him they shared the house with the spirit of its original owner, Hattie McCarver Babcock.

Charles Babcock, one of Oregon City's original treasurers, built the tall narrow house on Washington Street in 1892 for his young bride. The huge piece of land took up four city lots. Rumor has it that initially Hattie didn't want to move into the house because she believed her husband had built it with gambling winnings. She had no intention of living in a house that had been purchased with ill-gotten gains. Hattie stayed in the old house, at the other end of the property, even after the new home was finished, though she did finally relent and move in. She lived in the house until her death at age 84 in 1944.

Bette and Karl bought the heritage home in 1987. It sat empty for a couple of years, so they had plenty to fix and clean up in order to move in. The house had been one of the first in its time to be wired with electricity. When the Hayes moved in, they discovered that in addition to the vintage chandeliers hanging from the ceilings, much of the original wiring still hid behind the walls. In fact, some of the rooms had no wall switches at all. But the gardens, full of variegated red and white camellias, nevertheless bloomed profusely.

Shortly before moving in, an experience intimated that they might be sharing the house with an earthbound spirit. A spirit, unlike a ghost, is the living essence or soul of a person that has remained after death. Spirits, also unlike ghosts, are said to be able to communicate with the living. For example, if a person frequents a place where the deceased spent much of his or her time, a form of psychic communication can result. Hattie's spirit might still be connected to her home, and she may have used the flowers from her garden to convey a welcoming message.

Prior to the move, Karl often came to the house to work on things that needed fixing. He entered the house one day and discovered a freshly picked camellia blossom on the staircase of the empty house. At the time, he was the only person with a key. "He was sure no one brought it in," Bette told me. "He had locked the house when he left and no one had been there." Bette says Karl felt it was an indication that Hattie was happy to have them there. Bette herself was skeptical until she had her own inexplicable interaction with something or someone.

Karl was away on a hunting trip for the weekend. Bette was jolted out of a sound sleep by something hitting her back. At first she thought it was her cat Sassy, but then she remembered the cat was outside. Before going to bed, Bette had called her cat but it stubbornly refused to come in. Bette gave up and crawled into bed. Now she realized Sassy could not have pounced on her.

It was just before dawn. Nervous that a burglar might be in the house, Bette called a friend and told her that something had hit her so hard on the back it knocked the air out of her. "It really hit me hard," she recalls. She told her friend she was going to check for intruders and to call the police if she didn't call back in five minutes. The house was empty. And to this day Bette isn't sure if she was dreaming or if it was Hattie reminding her to let the cat back in.

Former Oregon City mayor Joan Cartales also lived in the house for three years. She noticed the scent of camellias would fill the rooms between November and January. During her stay there, from 1980 to 1983, most of Cartales' family met Mrs. Babcock. Her daughter was seven when she said a woman came to see her in the middle of the night. Her three-year-old son was terrified of some rooms. And a repairman was startled to see a woman pass him and continue down the hall while he was on his ladder.

Cartales told the *Oregonian* in 1996 that she and a friend actually saw Hattie Babcock. They were in the parlor and a woman dressed in a long, white gown with a high collar walked into the room. The scent of camellias accompanied the spirit. Not a word passed between Cartales and her friend until the ghost left. Upon comparing notes, they realized they had both seen the same thing.

Bette Hayes left the house reluctantly after 15 years. It was always a happy home for her and her family, but the house was just too big for her and her husband to manage. Before moving, she met Mrs. Babcock's granddaughter and other family members who called to ask if they might view the old homestead. "I never got a chance to ask them if they sensed their grandmother's presence," says Bette.

The End

Enjoy m~~ore haunting tales in these collecti~~ons by

GHOST HOUSE

GHOST HOUSE BOOKS

The colorful history of North America includes many spine-tingling tales of the supernatural. These fun, fascinating books by GHOST HOUSE BOOKS reveal the rich diversity of haunted places on the continent. Our ghostly tales involve well-known theatres, buildings and other landmarks, many of which are still in use. Collect the whole series!

Ghost Stories of America *by Dan Asfar and Edrick Thay*
A fascinating collection of frightening stories, culled from all 50 states and reflecting more than 200 years of haunted history. Visit famous haunts such as the Alamo, the Biltmore Hotel and Fort Laramie or learn about a ghost who may live in your neighborhood.
$11.95 US   ~~ISBN 1-894877-11-X~~

Ghost Storie
Ships, houses, ~~theatres an~~ ... ~~th~~e haunted
settings for this bone-chilling collection. A~~mong ... read~~ about a mountaineer ghost who warns hikers of a treacherous path, a spirit who inhabits Manresa Castle and ghosts of the Seattle Underground.
$10.95 US   ISBN 1-55105-260-1   5.25" x 8.25"   232 pages

Ghost Stories of California *by Barbara Smith*
The colorful history of California has given rise to a wealth of supernatural stories. This entertaining book includes tales about the ghostly sailors aboard the *Queen Mary*, the movie stars who never left the historic Hollywood Roosevelt Hotel and the infamous criminals still serving time in Alacatraz, America's most famous haunted prison.
$10.95 US   ISBN 1-55105-237-7   5.25" x 8.25"   224 pages

Ghost Stories of Michigan *by Dan Asfar*
This spirited collection features ghost stories from throughout the Great Lakes State, such as the Red Dwarf of Detroit, who turns up whenever tragedy visits, and the ghostly lighthouse keeper of White River, who continues to warn of danger.
$10.95 US   ISBN 1-894877-05-5   5.25" x 8.25"   224 pages

These and many more *Ghost Stories* books are available from your local bookseller or by ordering direct at 1-800-518-3541.